A Private and Public Faith

A PRIVATE
AND PUBLIC FAITH

by WILLIAM STRINGFELLOW

Reproduced by permission of
Wm. B. Eerdmans Publishing Co.

Wipf and Stock Publishers
150 West Broadway • Eugene OR 97401

1999

ISBN: 1-57910-215-8

Reprinted by *Wipf and Stock Publishers* 1999
150 West Broadway • Eugene OR 97401

Previously Published by Eerdmans

For ANDREW JAFFE

Preface

This is a tract. It consists of four essays about the status of religion in contemporary American society and about the condition of the churches of American Protestantism.

It is a tract, which means that it is polemical. It invites argument and controversy, not, however, for the sake of mere dispute, nor because of any overconfidence on my part in the observations made in the essays, but because of conviction that religion is, in principle, not only a very private matter but also a public issue, and because of conviction that the health and eventual maturity of the churches of American Protestantism depend upon getting some issues stated openly and discussed widely — by both clergy and laity and by the unchurched public as well.

It is a tract, which also means that it is in some degree a merely personal statement, based upon my own experiences and observations as a layman. I speak as a member of one of the churches, and as one who has had some glimpses of other churches in ecumenical activities and in other ways, but still as one without any specific vested interest in the enterprise of the churches, any of the churches, in America. That is to say, my livelihood does not depend upon the popularity or prosperity or good reputation of religion in any of its forms. My only interest in the subject — in the content and integrity of religion and of the churches — is not my livelihood, but my life. I care about the subject only insofar as it addresses my own life significantly, that is, at the level of my work as a lawyer and my participation in politics and my personal and private life. It is only if *that* is so that it becomes believable to me that the subject of religion bears significantly upon the lives and experiences of other men, and, therefore, of course, upon the relationships in which other men and I are exposed to each other both personally and in society.

7

As I find it, religion in America is characteristically atheistic or agnostic. Religion has virtually nothing to do with God and has little to do with the practical lives of men in society. Religion seems, mainly, to have to do with religion. The churches — particularly of Protestantism — in the United States are, to a great extent, preoccupied with religion rather than with the Gospel.

That, in brief, is the substance of the essays in this tract.

—WILLIAM STRINGFELLOW

Contents

The Folly of Religion

See to it that no one makes a prey of you by philosophy and empty deceit, according to human tradition, according to the elemental spirits of the universe, and not according to Christ.

Colossians 2:8

FOR THE CHRISTIAN FAITH, the happiest thing to happen in America for a long time is the recession in religion. For the churches in the United States, the healthiest fact at the present time is the decline of religion.

The so-called religious revival appears to be over. The proportion of the general population maintaining some religious affiliation is down from what it was a few years ago. Reports from the universities and colleges indicate a growing indifference toward organized religious programs on the campuses. Fewer people are going to church services. Sales of religious books have dropped. Seminary enrollment has fallen off. Within the churches, and notably among the clergy, there is evidence of restiveness, disillusionment, and even cynicism about the ecclesiastical institutions.

It is just as well. The religious revival was no return to the Gospel anyway, and, though it enriched some churches in both numbers and assets, it was no renewal of the Church. While it lasted, it was part of a great post-war inflation of American life, affording to the nation a benediction for ascendant American power and wealth in the midst of the world's poverty, impotence, and want. The religious revival reflected the fat of post-war America. And while the religious revival contributed to the concealment of the interior decadence of American society, it at the same time beguiled many folk into thinking that personal satisfaction or success or security are synonyms for righteousness. The religious revival offered people a plenary indulgence.

11

All of this would not be distressing for Christians if it could be simply construed as a temporary and passing aberration in the religious experience of American society. But I, for one, fear that it was not so; on the contrary, the postwar religious revival represented an outburst of allegiance to and acclaim for what are deeply imbedded notions about religion in the American mentality. And more specifically, one suspects that the religious revival was a response to and exploitation of the self-confidence, sense of destiny, and realization of power that marked post-war America, a response nourished by an idea of religion which American Protestantism, at least, had harbored for generations. It is not so much, in other words, that Christians might be or should be offended or disturbed by the religious views asserted within the context of the religious revival — though that is a serious consideration — but that the religious understanding embodied in the revival, for all its variety — from Norman Peale to Billy Graham to Oral Roberts, has been latent both in doctrine and practice in American Protestantism all along but erupted notoriously and commercially and in popularized fashion only during the post-war years. In one sense, even, Christians can be thankful that there has been this revival in religion in America, if only because in it the surface of Protestantism was scratched and what was there — right under the surface — was exposed.

The question now is whether anything deeper remains to be exposed. The question now is whether Protestantism in America, which more than any other of the churches was the sponsor of the religious revival, will now be also the principal victim in the demise of the revival. The issue is this: If the religious revival finds its ideational roots in the American experience as a pluralistic society, and if Protestantism in America so readily and uncritically became the chief sponsor of that revival and these ideas of religion, and if the revival now collapses, does Protestantism in America have the faith, integrity, stamina, or relevance to survive? After the frustration, error, and chaos nourished by the religious revival in both personal and public life in this country, and to which Protestantism, to a very great extent, committed itself, has Protestantism anything else to say or to represent in American society? What vacuum exists in the churches of America which enabled Protestantism to so readily and uncritically accommodate itself to the heresies capitalized and popularized and merchandized in the religious revival? Is it possible, now that the revival falters and wanes, for Protestants to extricate themselves from the religious practices and thoughts represented in the revival? Or has Protestantism in America just simply and radically dissociated itself from the Gospel, and has the climax of that action been the religious revival which now is defunct? How far have the strange shibboleths spawned in the American pluralistic experience infected Protestantism? Or do American Protestants much care anyway what they believe, or what the Church is, or how the Gospel relates to contemporary American life, so long as the institutional existence of the churches is protected and the churches retain an amiable reputation in the community? If the public idols of the recent religious revival are repudiated, or what is more likely, just increasingly neglected and ignored by society, does American Protestantism have anything, or, more precisely, any One to offer or commend as replacement, or will Protestantism retract and conserve and wait until attracted by some idol in the offing? In short, does American Protestantism want merely to be, as it has largely been during the so-called revival, not to mention the times before that, the religious disguise and aura of American society, or does it want to serve and uphold the Gospel in this society even in the face of the radical and historic hostility of American society toward the Gospel?

Through what can only be the irony of God's grace, after the years of guilty association between American Protestantism and the religious revival, Protestantism here has the chance to acknowledge and answer such questions. And the very life of American Protestantism as, in any Biblical, historic, and coherent sense, a Christian community, depends upon the answers, apart, of course, from the further patience

of God with those whom He calls to His service — publicans
and sinners, generally — and puts in His service in this world.

The crucial question to be asked about American Protestantism is whether it has become so radically degenerate
as a Christian community, as Church, and so fearful of the
news which the Church bears in the world that in the main
it now amounts only to another religious institution and
cultus, with no more to distinguish or commend itself than
any other religious views or exercises. The crisis is the real
possibility that Protestantism has become mere religion.

Permit a more personal word, before going any further,
about this issue.

Personally, I find no cause to be interested in mere religion.
It can be a certain diversion, I admit, to speculate and
argue about religious ideas and practices, but I am no longer
in college, and my law practice does not often permit the
luxury of hypothetical and speculative matters. It appears to
me more urgent and more necessary to deal with history, that
is, with actual life as it has preceded the present time, and
with the actual life of the present time. So I do not bother,
as far as I am aware, with dabbling in religion. And if, as it
may in my own lifetime turn out, Protestantism — like
Zen, or "religious science," or the other sects — is or becomes
only an institution of religion devoted to its own maintenance
and a practice of religion for its own sake, then I am just not
superstitious enough to remain a Protestant.

But when, now and then, I turn to and listen to the Bible,
or when, now and then, I hear the Word of God exposed
in preaching, or when, now and then, I see the Gospel represented in the Holy Communion and I thereupon become
a participant in and witness of the real life which is given to
the world, or when, now and then, I meet some Christian,
or when, now and then, I discern and encounter the presence
of God's Word in the ordinary affairs of everyday existence
in the world — on these occasions, in these circumstances, I
am reminded, if sometimes ruefully, that the Gospel is no
mere religion in *any* essential respect.

For in any of these circumstances, on any of these occasions, what is emphatic and lucid and — best of all — *true* is that this Gospel of Jesus Christ ends all religious speculation; demolishes all merely religious ceremonies and sacrifices appeasing unknown gods; destroys every exclusiveness which religion attaches to itself in God's name; attests that the presence of God is not remote, distant, and probably out-of-reach — but here, now, and with us in this world, already. This Gospel means that the very life of God is evident in this world, in this life, because Jesus Christ once participated in the common life of men in the history of our world.

The Christian faith is distinguished, diametrically, from mere religion, in that religion begins with the proposition that some god exists; Christianity, meanwhile, is rejoicing in God's manifest presence among us. Religion describes men, mind you, usually sincere and honorable and intelligent men, searching for God, or, more characteristically, searching for some substitute for God — that is, some idea of what God may be like — or would be like — and then worshipping that idea and surrounding that substitution with dogma and discipline. But the Gospel tells when and how and why and where God has sought us and found us and offered to take us into His life. Religion is the attempt to satisfy the curiosity of men in this world about God; Jesus Christ is the answer to the curiosity of men in this world about what it means to be truly a man in this world which God created. Religion is fulfilled, always, in one of two ways: either (1) in consecrating some object or power or ideology or man — or, in earlier days, some commodity or natural phenomenon or animal or any thing — as a god, and as, hopefully, *the god*, or (2) in projecting god beyond history, into the unknown and the unknowable, enthroned, perhaps, before this life or in some after life but never in *this* life, out of this world, oblivious of the present existence and grandly indifferent to it, abstract, irrelevant, impotent, indifferent — a ridiculous god, in fact, no god at all.

So, just personally, religion does not particularly intrigue me, though the Gospel does. Religion does not address my practical, everyday, working life, but the Gospel does. I do not care — I do not mean to be impudent, but I, for one, do not care — if God lives somewhere and someplace else. But I care a lot when I hear — in the Bible, or in the Church, or in the presence of a Christian, or in the ordinary happenings of my own life — that God is with us now, anyway and already, and even, thank God, before we call upon Him. I care a lot, in other words, when I hear the news of Jesus Christ, because it is a different news than I receive when I encounter the various religions.

Part of the difference is, obviously, the news that God (even) cares for me (even). All those smaller gods — the gods of the various religions — are indifferent to that. What they care about, what idols are concerned with — is whether they are worshipped, is whether their own existence is verified and lauded. But Christ speaks very differently. Indeed, Christ embodies the difference between religion and the Gospel. Christ bespeaks the care of God for everything to do with actual life, with life as it is lived by anybody and everybody day in and day out. Christ bespeaks *my* life: in all its detail and mistake and humor and fatigue and surprise and contradiction and freedom and ambiguity and quiet and wonder and sin and peace and vanity and variety and lust and triumph and defeat and rest and love and all the rest that it is from time to time; and, cheer up, with *your* life, just as much, in as full intimacy, touching your whole biography, abiding every secret, *with you*, whoever, wherever you are, any time, any place. Christ bespeaks the destinies of nations, and all the lesser principalities and powers, the corporations and universities and unions and utilities and the whole frighteningly complex constellation of authorities which assert themselves in the day-to-day life of the world.

In short, religion supposes that God is yet to be discovered; Christianity knows that God has already come among us. Religious speculation suspects there is God, somewhere, sometime; the Gospel reports His presence and action in this world even in those circumstances within which we are unaware of Him. Religion suppresses the truth, because the truth obviates religion.

The religious suppose that only the religious know about God or care about God, and that God cares only for the religious. Characteristically, religion is precious and possessive toward God, and institutes and conducts itself as if God really needs religion, as if His existence depends upon the recognition of religion. Religion considers that God is a secret disclosed only in the discipline and practice of religion. But all this is most offensive to the Word of God. The best news of God is that He is no secret. The news of God embodied in Jesus Christ is that God is openly and notoriously active in the world. In this news the Christian Church is constituted; it is this news which the Christian Church exists to spread. Where the Church, however, asserts that God is hidden in or behind creed or ceremony — even those which are decent and which God gladly receives and blesses — or where God is thought to be confined to the sanctuary, then in such events the Christian Church, forsaking the good news of God's presence in history, becomes a vulgar imitation of mere religion. The Church, where faithful to the news, is not the place where men come to seek God; on the contrary, the Church is just the place where men gather to declare that God takes the initiative in seeking men. The Church, unlike any religion, exists to present to the world and to celebrate in the world, and on behalf of the world, God's presence and power and utterance and action in the on-going life of the world.

God's presence and action in common life means that it is possible that a man know something of God — something beyond speculation and surmise — something quite concrete and certain — something, also, immediately, intimately and truly personal. God's witness to Himself in history encompasses His specific grace and action in your own life and mine. I may be regular in church attendance. I may become more or less learned in the doctrine and history of the Church. I may honor saints. I may yield to the authority and wisdom of the Church's teaching. I may find fellowship and concern in the Church. I may listen to the preachers. But none of these are the same as knowledge of God. The possibility that I know anything of God originates in His first coming to me, in His first knowing me. I may know God only because He knows me, knows me with the familiarity of One who has made another, knows me in my creation, knows me, as well, in every time and place, knows me in my death. The possibility of my faith belongs to His existence. The opportunity for faith is given in His initiative toward me, or any other man. Faith in God begins and is sustained in and consummated in the fidelity of God to His own creation. Faith in God — in God, that is, not in religion and not in some doctrine about God, however venerable or, indeed, however correct — is, in other words, a work of the Holy Spirit — of the living and contemporary presence of God in the world — in which my life, once lost, is found and returned to me by God.

The news of God's presence in real, everyday life, the word that God is living and is not some abstract power, the truth that He is in this world and not outside it, the fact that God makes Himself known in history, the possibility of knowledge of God which is offered to men in Jesus Christ — all of this runs counter to American ideas of religion and of the function of religion in society. A statement and examination of the religious notions commonly recited in America will help to demonstrate how radically offensive they are to the Gospel and will show, too, how far Protestantism has become committed to these ideas in place of the Gospel.

The Religiosity of Religion

The central idea about religion in America is that religion has only to do with religion, not with life. This notion originated, in part, from the great anxiety in early America to avoid those debilitating religious controversies which divide and corrupt the national life, and the persecutions in the name of religion which had induced some of the settlers of the country to flee Europe. Religion here was to be a personal and optional matter, and the way to insure that freedom was to constitutionally forbid the establishment of any religion and to maintain a separation of church and state.[1]

Meanwhile, among American Protestants, the Reformation principle of dissent and of the integrity of the relationship between God and a man was transmuted into a radical individualism which made each man the author of his own religion. For more than a century and a half, Protestantism has nurtured this notion of autonomous and personal religiosity, and this notion, more than any other single factor, explains the grotesque division, separation, and segregation of the Church in the United States and the stifling religious ethos in which Christians in America find themselves today.

As accommodating as it may seem to be for a pluralistic society, this American idea of religion is openly hostile to the Biblical description of the Church as the Body of Christ living in the midst of the traffic and turmoil and conflict of the world on behalf of the world. The Biblical image of the Church is, to be sure, that of a stranger and alien in the world, despised by the nation, but the Biblical image of the Church is *never* one of an innocuous, isolationist religious society cut off from the actual affairs of men and nations in the world.

This desperate and lonely and unloving religiosity, this American persuasion that religion has to do with religion and not with the world, is deeply appealing to the mentality of the American people, both within and outside the churches. It emerged in the 1960 presidential campaign, where all the candidates recited that the historic separation of church and state in America means that religion and politics are separated in principle. And if religion and politics are separated and are to have nothing to do with each other, then religion and practical life are separated. And though this view is mani-

---

1. For a more extensive discussion of this, see "Law, Polity, and the Reunion of the Church," *Ohio State Law Journal,* August, 1960; *The Ecumenical Review,* April, 1961, p. 287.

festly repugnant to the Gospel, and offensive to the ministry of Christ, virtually the whole American ecclesiastical leadership remained silent on the issue.

The separation of religion from the practical affairs of society is a convenient doctrine for those who fear that social change would threaten or modify their own political or economic or social self-interest. Typically, here, it takes the form of the argument that religion should not be controversial, that it is about different and higher and otherworldly things, and that religion should be kept out of issues about which it has nothing to do or say and about which it knows nothing. Religion, it is insisted, is for the sanctuary, not the marketplace. This has long been the line of economic conservatives in this country opposed to everything from the income tax to social security. It is currently the appeal being made by the medical profession's lobby through doctors prominent in their denominations with the aim to deter church assemblies from advocating medical care for the aged. It is among the arguments of some of the segregationists seeking both to forestall any significant entry of the churches into the struggle for integration in American public life and also to preserve as long as possible segregation within the churches, in congregations and in church-related institutions.

If it is any comfort to such extremists, let it be recorded here that the same conviction can be found elsewhere, too — for example, among impoverished negroes in some of the southern negro congregations. I was associated with the defense counsel in the cases of the fifteen Episcopal Church clergy who were arrested in Jackson, Mississippi, in September, 1961, when they attempted to pass through Jackson enroute to the General Convention of the Episcopal Church in Detroit. They were engaged, not in a Freedom Ride, but in a prayer pilgrimage, in visiting church-related schools and other institutions in both the South and the North which still cling to segregation or discrimination in one form or another. Their bus route took them through Jackson, and when they tried to have lunch in the restaurant in Jackson's bus terminal, they were arrested shortly before their bus was scheduled to leave and charged with conduct which might provoke a breach of the peace. Eventually, these priests were legally exonerated, the State of Mississippi having failed to prove that their conduct justified the arrests.[2] On the day in which the cases were dismissed, an invitation came to us to visit that evening a "mass meeting" in the Negro neighborhood in Jackson. The meeting, as it happened, was to be in a Negro congregation where no similar meeting had apparently ever been held before. When we arrived at the church we discovered an argument taking place among some of the elders of the congregation about whether the meeting should be permitted to take place. Those opposed to permitting it contended, typically, that the church was a place reserved for preaching and prayer and must not be used for politics and controversy. As it turned out, no meeting was held — those believing that religion is isolated from practical life prevailed. And in that they echoed the sentiment of hosts of laity, clergy, and ecclesiastics in the Episcopal Church around the country who had been scandalized by and vehementally critical of the prayer pilgrimage which these priests had undertaken.

Such people — if their profession of the Christian faith is serious — must answer this question: What is there to pray about in church if the Church is not the place where men ought to intercede for those who are sick or bereft or suffering or imprisoned or in any need in the world? And how can the Word of God be preached at all where it does not expose every man and nation to the judgment and grace of the Word? And how can God be worshipped as God, save in the certainty of His care for the whole of life — with all the controversy and tension and conflict and passion which mark the ordinary existence of men in society?

Ironically, of course, those most eager and apt to counsel — in the name of religion — the abstension of the Church from

2. These cases against the priests were dismissed on May 21, 1962. On September 10, four of the clergy filed suit in the Federal District Court in Jackson against the arresting police officers for false arrest.

public life, those, that is, who claim that the only proper province of religion is religion, are those who in fact call upon this doctrine about religion as a safeguard for their own position in society. So long as religion is quiet about society it upholds whatever is the prevailing *status quo* in society. But if one benefits, or is persuaded that he benefits, from the preservation of the *status quo,* then so long as religion remains aloof from society, it is not controversial. It is only when religion disrupts or threatens one's self-interest that it is condemned as controversial.

In the eyes of the Christian faith, by contrast, no state of society can ever prevail, in the past or now or in the future, which satisfies the concern of Christians for the world. The Christian is committed permanently to radical protest in society. He is always dissatisfied with the existing state of affairs. He is always representing, on behalf of all men, a fulfillment of life transcending the fragile and conflicting and ambiguous aspirations of men for their common life in the world.

The idea that religion has to do only with religion is not simply the view of extremists, opportunists, fanatics, paranoids or presidential candidates. Masses of solid, respectable, moderate folk who are members and leaders and clergy of the major churches of American Protestantism fondly cling to this doctrine, the doctrine which severs religion from life. How often is it preached — instead of the Gospel — from the pulpit in your congregation? How often is it the substance of the Sunday School lesson? How many members of your congregation think that their religion is a precious, private, personal possession protected from, and in turn shielding them from, the crude, harsh, cruel actualities of life? How many of you know so little of the Bible and consider the Gospel so carelessly and frivolously that you think it has nothing to do with your own practical life, much less with the lives of your enemies, or of other men, or with the lives of nations? How often does the separation of religion and life, of the Gospel and the world, of theology and existence appear as the bulwark of American Protestantism?

One test of how far this notion has invaded and corrupted the churches of Protestantism is the extent to which the time, wealth, energy and resources of the churches are committed merely to the maintenance of the churches institutionally. Anyone who has served on a church board or worked in a denominational headquarters or been active in a council of churches or served as a parish minister knows the answer to that. The churches of Protestantism, in the main, are committed primarily, where not exclusively, to housekeeping, to preserving and maintaining premises for religious exercises and recitations. Examine, sometime, a budget of a congregation. It goes for the upkeep of the plant and the salaries of the clergy, with perhaps a nominal sum for missions. But where is the concern of the congregation for the life of the world represented? If it is not reflected in the financial operation of a congregation, will it be really encompassed in the worship of the congregation? Or listen to the complaints of those who work in some of the great ecclesiastical bureaucracies in the churches, and find out from them how much of their time is expended in conference with their colleagues in discussion of a task in which, then, they have no time to engage. The institutional apparatus of the American churches has grown so overweighted and cumbersome, the attrition within these institutions has become so exhaustive and self-defeating, that even in a parish, to say nothing of the church headquarters, the churches are in reality almost wholly committed to serving their own existence. In such circumstances, religion, not only ideologically, but empirically, has only to do with religion, but not with life.

Sometimes, of course, it is acknowledged in the churches that religion has to do with certain limited aspects of life, that is, with some decisions of behavior in a man's personal and family life. Religion then is thought of as providing a personal ethics for prudential conduct. But religion then becomes a scheme embracing, defining, and informing merely personal morality. Religion then is the index of what is right and what is wrong, if not in public life, at least in private life. Religion then is aimed at assuring the adherent of religion of his own moral rectitude by equipping him with the moral information with and within which to make his decisions in personal life.

Yet if the content of religion is no more than that, then I am inclined to go along with the remarks attributed to Mrs. Kennedy, the President's wife, who, when asked to comment during the presidential campaign on the controversy about religion and politics, allowed that religion was very important in personal life and very good for children, but that it ought not to be introduced into politics. If religion offers only some advice or instruction relevant to personal behavior, if it has nothing to do with politics and the public life of society, then, while it may still in fact be good for children, it is not good for me. If religion is only that, it has not the dignity to claim my life.

It has not the dignity to claim my life because my life — just as that of any man — is such that the issues of personal behavior cannot be extricated and neatly isolated from the life of society. Politics and work impinge upon the most apparently private matters. Peace, and war, and the racial crisis, and urbanization, and all the great issues affect the daily existence of ordinary people. It is not so much, mind you, that ordinary people have, even in American democracy, much of any influence or control over such issues, but more that the practical lives of people are confined, directed, and shaped by the conflicts in the world among the powers and authorities of ideology and race and nation. Religion which attempts to isolate and shield private life from the rest of the life of the world, although it may contain the comfort of escape, the illusion of security, and the pride of pietism, is essentially a fraud, and, in any event, alien to the Gospel with its passion for the whole life of the world as it is.

Such religion, too, grossly oversimplifies the reality of moral conflict in the world, including moral conflict within the private life of a man. Religion of this sort fails to apprehend the intense ambiguity of moral decision. This variety of religion contends that it is possible for a man, in the sphere of his own immediate affairs, to discern what is right and wrong, and to implement a decision so informed with more or less discipline. But the truth is that the extent of any man's insight into what is good or bad reaches only to that which is advantageous to himself. A man may, indeed, be able to figure out what is good, or bad, for him or for his family. But that which is good for him, is bad for some one else, and, in principle, for *everyone* else in the world. The intensity and complexity of moral conflict is the assertion and pursuit of each man's own self-interest as over against that of every other man.

To ordain and dignify personal self-interest as morally correct in any essential and ultimate sense is a very great arrogance. And from the point of view of the Christian faith, it is very perilous. For what a man who practices this sort of religion is really saying is that he can second-guess how God will judge him in respect to the decision or course of action which he now undertakes and which he claims is morally right. It is the essence of human sin for man to boast of the power to discern what is good and what is evil, and thus to be like God.[3] I think men must foreswear such presumption and wait upon the last embarrassing day when all the secrets will be exposed and God judges every act and word of every man. Meanwhile, it surely does not influence or appease God for men to disguise their bondage to the power of sin as religion.

The notion that religion has to do only with religion, or the mutation of that view which encompasses only personal morality within the sphere of religion, is characteristically associated in America with forms either of agnosticism or of atheism. And both are popular among Protestants.

The Agnosticism of Religion

Agnosticism asserts that knowledge of God is impossible. The religion prevalent in much of American Protestantism is

3. Cf. Genesis 3:5.

essentially agnostic. The mere practice of religion has become the substitute for the Gospel, that is, for the knowledge of God which God Himself gives to men in Jesus Christ. Perhaps American Protestantism just does not want the Gospel anyway. Perhaps it wants what it has instead.

In many of the churches of Protestantism, as has already been observed, the acknowledgement and reliance upon God's initiative in making Himself known in the world has been forsaken for a religion defined in terms of prudential ethics, and religion provides the moral sanction for each person to pursue that which will preserve his own life as over against that of everybody else.

The most popular version of this during the religious revival was, of course, distilled in the cult of "positive thinking" in which the uses of religion are appropriated for the aggrandizement of whatever interest or objective the practitioner of religion wishes to attain or acquire. This is religion that "works" — it can be an affirmative factor in sales promotion, it can provide the stimulus to business success, it can help ball players to hit home runs — there is no end to its power and ability to get results. Usually the results that it gets enrich the religionist or appease his ambitions, but always there is silence in this religion about those who may be victims of the success or fame or wealth of the faithful.

A year or two ago I spent some time in Haiti and had the opportunity there to observe some primitive Voodoo, which is still practiced there. It is an enchanting religion, succeeding, as it apparently does, in providing ecstatic preoccupation for folk who otherwise know only squalor, hunger, political bondage, and grotesque poverty. Voodoo in Haiti is an exotic mixture of indigenous African religion and Freemasonry. The Haitians have aptly associated these, intuiting the superstition, caste, escapism, and ritualism common to both. Essentially the practice of Voodoo, as I observed it, consists of ritualistic repetitions which induce in the priest and the participants that state of being they wish were true. Usually in Haiti it is some erotic experience which is sought. And if, in this religion, that is sought with enough conviction and persistence, even to the point of frenzy, then, lo! it comes to pass. It is, I suppose, a practice of auto-suggestion or self-hypnotism. It is, in fact, a very highly developed and sophisticated form of what in America is called "positive thinking."

One somehow admires Voodoo more than positive thinking, not only because it is clearly a more advanced and more esoteric religion, but also because the Haitians not only think their positive thoughts but commit their whole beings — their voices and bodies as well as their thoughts and emotions — into this practice, whereas their American counterparts concentrate on the development only of an aggressive will power. And if the Voodoo religionists are carnal and lusty, at least their lusts are not so mundane as selling more encyclopedias or merchandising mustard seeds.

That positive thinking so typically focuses upon personal security and success is not surprising when one considers the extent to which Protestantism in America has become the sponsor of the familiar doctrines of free enterprise and individual initiative. Not only rural Protestantism, but also Protestantism in the city — what is left of it — has become a make-believe haven where the individual is exalted, where religion is meant to confirm and appease his desires and ambitions, where the individual controls his own destiny, where the only limits on a man are said to be those native to his own mentality, volition, health, competitive spirit and luck, where those that get ahead deserve it, and where God is eager to help those who help themselves. But in this enchanting sanctuary there is hardly a whisper about the praise of the Lord our God, or the remembrance of the poor, or loving an enemy, or giving away one's life and in that way finding it, or the passion of Christ, or the power of the Resurrection, or the discernment of God's presence in the world, or the jubilance and surprise of the Eucharist, or the earnest expectancy of the Last Day of God's judgment and mercy.

The replacement of the knowledge of God with the mere practice of religion is curiously present, too, in the mass evangelism which achieved such notoriety during the religious revival, although it must be acknowledged that the mass evangelists bespoke a regard for the Bible which is to be commended at a time when so much of Protestantism has abandoned the Bible, especially in preaching, worship, and what is called "Christian education." Nevertheless, the central appeal of the mass evangelists was one of a radically individualistic religion, and in some instances there was open disdain for the Church as the Body of Christ in the world, as the holy community serving the world in the name of Christ. Here the emphasis is upon dignifying human sin as that which is responsible for the fallenness of not only men but the rest of Creation as well. So if men's work is harsh and burdensome, or if the authorities and principalities are relentless and oppressive, it is the fault of men and the consequence of sin. Are politics corrupt? Is alcoholism increasing? Is there scandal in the great corporations as well as in the unions? Does the nation's prestige decline? Are there more traffic fatalities? Does juvenile delinquency plague society? Is America losing the cold war? Is it all because of the lusts of men. It is all because of individual sin. Repent. It will all change if enough repent. This is the stock merchandise of Protestant evangelism. Aside from other criticisms of this kind of religion, one trouble with it is that to extol the power of human sin, and particularly the efficacy of an individual's sin, is another way of asserting the dominion of men in the world. The focus of this religion is not the initiative of God in history but the practice of religion by the individual in some singular, stereotyped act of personal volition and emotion by which a desired result can be achieved. This is a kind of inverse "positive thinking," and, one suspects, this is "positive thinking" for the lower classes.

In between these extremes of Protestantism, there is another version of the agnosticism of religion. It consists of a social gospel which, though more chastened and cautious now than a generation or so ago, and though more orthodox in its vocabulary (that is, nowadays Jesus is being called Jesus Christ instead of just Jesus), still expects that fortunate concurrence of circumstances in which men master history and build themselves a city of salvation. For such Protestants sacramental worship seems an indecisive, historically insignificant, and archaic exercise. And why shouldn't it if, from their vantage point, the saving work of God in Jesus Christ is incomplete and still contingent upon the work of men, and God is less than God? These are the Protestants who cannot, in other words, comprehend why the Gospel narrative does not end in the political triumph of Palm Sunday, not realizing that the event of Palm Sunday repeats in the life of Christ His temptation by the Devil in the wilderness. Consequently, of course, they cannot come to terms with the treachery of Judas and the apostasy of the rest of the disciples, nor countenance the Crucifixion, nor believe the descent into Hell, nor consider the Resurrection from the dead anything but an embarrassing hyperbole.

The Atheism of Religion

The denunciation of the knowledge of God which is agnosticism, and which appears in various guises in American Protestantism, is not the only affliction visited upon the churches in the United States, nor the only form in which the hostility between American religious notions and the Gospel is evident.

Perhaps the most radical conflict between the American religious ethos and the Christian faith emerges from the proposition that in a society like the United States, within which there is a multiplicity of sects and churches and religious groups, it is not significant what a man believes religiously, or whether he is affiliated with any religious society or any denomination, so long as whatever his religious position is, he adheres to it sincerely. It is not the content of religious belief or confession which is important, but the heartiness with which the adherent believes whatever it is he professes to believe. Faith, in this way, becomes faith in faith, not faith in God, nor even faith in some abstractions or hypotheses about God.

Sometimes, somewhat paradoxically, this idea is coupled with praise of the religious origins of American society, the common talk of Americans as a deeply religious people, and reference to vague spiritual values to which the nation is just as vaguely committed. Such an instance took place during the 1960 presidential campaign when Mr. Nixon indicated that though, of course, religion should not influence politics, the American people were after all an essentially religious folk who would not care to elect a President who had no religion. One must have some religion, though it doesn't really matter what it is.

Religion, in such a view, becomes a wholly subjective thing, looking for its content, if it has any, to the imagination, intelligence, innovation of the believer. Consequently, religion, in this sense, is an utterly erratic thing, the content of which changes from one time to another and from what one man says to what another man says. Religion, then, becomes indeed all things to all men simultaneously.

But to imply that all religion is the same, that all religion is completely contingent upon the one who believes, is tantamount to atheism. It is quite the same thing as saying that there is no God — at least no God who may be known, no living God; that there is no historically active God who has His own presence, apart from whether or not His presence is acknowledged; no God who has His own integrity, apart from minds or feelings of men; no God who has His own identity, apart from the existence of men; no God whose mode of action is consistent and faithful and ubiquitous in the world and which may be beheld and to which men may respond in one way or another. The man who declares that it makes no difference what you believe so long as you believe something is declaring that there is no truth, that there is no ultimate meaning which has immediate and concrete significance for the world, that there is no God.

Christians, at least in Protestantism in America, have been intimidated far too long by this idea. It is argued that this is the American conception, one which safeguards religious freedom and that it is anyway pragmatically essential to harmony among the diverse religious groups in society. The argument wears thin, however, in the face of the experience of other democratic societies — Britain and Scandinavia and Western Europe — where the public freedom to practice religions of various kinds appears not to be abridged by the existence of established churches. If this doctrine is, in fact, a safeguard for the public freedom of religious practice, it is at least not the only one imaginable or available within the democratic tradition. And at what price is this alleged harmony accomplished if in fact the doctrine upon which it rests requires of religious folk a profession, in effect, of atheism?

Insofar as American Protestantism begins now, in the ecumenical discussions with Roman Catholic and Orthodox and Anglican Christians, to remember something of the corporate existence of the Church, something of the Oneness and Holiness of the Body of Christ, it must necessarily and inevitably abandon its historic association — its guilty association — with the radical individualism which has so dominated its thought and organization and way of life in the United States. The auspices which Protestantism has provided for the notions that all religion is the same, and that each individual is an authoritative arbiter of religious truth, have inhibited evangelism in the name of the Church, have jeopardized prophetic witness, and have gravely corrupted the corporate worship of Christians. Moreover, the accommodation of Protestantism to these American religious notions has impaired the responsibility of the Protestant churches to undertake any critical stance in relation to the nation and to American society.

The freedom of Christians to serve the world in the proclamation and celebration of the Gospel, in the presentation and representation of the Gospel in the midst of secular life, is a freedom given to the Church in the covenant between God and men, namely, baptism. That is a peculiar freedom, one in which Christians individually and as the Body of Christ are secured from the power of death and from all the lesser powers and authorities which, in the name of death, purport to reign in this world. It is a strong and splendid freedom not contingent upon *any* political arrangements between the Church, or the churches, and the nation at any time. There never is any political situation, whether past or present, whether modern totalitarian societies or democratic states, upon which the effective exercise by Christians of the freedom given to them in the Gospel to proclaim and honor the Gospel is in the slightest dependent. And although the public freedom for the practice of religion which is constitutionally sanctioned in the United States is an important convenience to the churches and sects, it is not indispensable to the freedom of Christians to represent the Gospel established and given to Christians in the Gospel itself. The problem for American Protestants is to avoid cherishing the first freedom so much that they foreswear the second.

If in America Protestants or other Christians exercise their freedom in the Gospel to proclaim the Gospel, they are apt to be disruptive of the superficial harmony which is asserted to exist and to be essential for the good order and peace of society. So be it. The health and maturity of a democratic society is not determined by the absence or suppression of conflict and controversy, by any apparent tranquility concealing all the contention and difference and diversity within society; on the contrary, this maturity is exhibited by the open and candid disclosure of difference and conflict and the resolution of controversy within the rule of law. It is not the ignoring of fear or conflict which is characteristic of a mature democracy, but the capability and way of adjudicating conflict. This easy-going, genial, cheap comity so prevalent and popular in American life is no strength, but a weakness in the nation. And Protestants should be the last — although they have been among the first — to accommodate themselves to such a truce in American religious life. In any case, in America or anywhere else, Christians cannot be parties to a truce founded upon the assertion that it matters not what a man believes; rather, they must refute that sort of atheism with the boldness and scandal of their faith in Jesus Christ.

The Specter of Protestantism

*If with Christ you died to the elemental spirits of the universe,
why do you live as if you still belonged to the world?*

Colossians 2:20

EVEN INSOFAR AS PROTESTANTISM in America has not been
entrapped in the religiosity and agnosticism or atheism of
religion, the churches of Protestantism are beset by terrible
confusions about the nature of the Church and the mission
of the Church in the world.

Jacques Ellul, the French lawyer and theologian, in a
conversation a few years ago, said that the dilemma for Christians in France nowadays is this, that on the one hand, the
churches there are so debilitated and apostate that a Christian
can hardly bear to remain in a church, and yet, on the other
hand, no Christian can leave a church lest he fail to confess
his own part of the responsibility for the very conditions in
a church which provoke protest.[1] At the time Ellul said
this, I told him that I did not observe that the situation
in the churches in the United States was as yet so acute and
poignant. But, now, a few years and some second thoughts
later, I conclude that Ellul describes the problem here in
America as well.

At the same time, a word of caution now needs very much
to be added. Within the churches, and, I observe, particularly
within the seminaries and among younger clergy, it becomes
common to complain caustically and even cynically about the
state of the contemporary churches. And while I have not
been exactly shy in my own protests, either in my own congregation or in the churches at large, and though I am
sympathetic to the frustration and disillusionment of the
clergy and others, and while I think that there can be no

1. See Jacques Ellul, *The Presence of the Kingdom.*

tolerance of the superstitions and outright heresies that infect much of the lives of the churches and that these must be radically excised — or perhaps more appropriately exorcised — for all of that it must be remembered that complaint is not a remedy, and that protest is only the invocation of reform. Let none, in other words, outside the churches complain, for only those within the churches know the agony and burden of the disunity, corruption, and weakness of the churches. And let those within the churches act as boldly as they speak lest their reluctance or timidity in acting aggravate further that against which they speak.

Let it be remembered, too, that God does not need the churches. The concern for the purity, fidelity, and unity of the churches as the Church originates in the need of the churches of God, not the other way around. God makes His own witness in the world, and makes that witness even in the very weakness of the churches which are affronts to His name. This was shown to me when I was living in East Harlem. A law student came one day to me to ask if he could assist in any way in my law practice in that neighborhood. He was no Christian, nor even much religious. One of his parents was a non-religious Jew, the other a non-religious Protestant — or so he described them. In the months that followed, he and I talked a good deal — about law and the city and politics and clowns and poetry and death and other such important things. I do not recollect that we ever talked about God plainly and openly, although, in a sense, we really talked only of God. And the Church was never mentioned in our conversations, although he knew that I am a member of the Church. Then one Saturday evening — it was the eve of Pentecost, though I do not know if he knew that — he called me and asked if he could go with me to church the next morning. We went to an early celebration of the Holy Communion at the congregation of which I was then a member. Now it was the custom in this parish to hear a homily from the minister presiding at the Eucharist. There was one that day. I remember that it was gruesome, and though the word "Pentecost" was mentioned now and then during the sermon, the sermon was not about Pentecost: the remarks that were made were not about the Word of God at all.

Eventually, the service ended and my guest and I went to have some coffee. "I think we have to go back," he decided. I asked him why, and he told me, "Because you didn't participate in that service at all." He was right, of course; I hadn't. I had been distracted by what had happened in this homily, and I was ashamed of what had happened in this church when my friend, this stranger to the Church, had been present, and I had been preoccupied during most of the service following the homily with thoughts of what an awful and misleading impression he would receive of the Church and, indeed, of the Gospel, from his visit to a congregation. And so, we tried again.

We went to the late service at the same congregation. It was still Pentecost, but it turned out also to be the anniversary of the establishment of the parish, and it was the more recent anniversary that was observed. There were a lot of words recited — it seemed at every available intermission in the service — about the historic importance of the parish anniversary. There was a special hymn which had been commissioned for the occasion and which resembled a college *alma mater* song. And there was a guest preacher, an illustrious one, one whom upon other occasions I have heard preach the Gospel. He did not do so that day. He did not acknowledge Pentecost, nor even, except for an introductory pleasantry, the much celebrated parish anniversary. Instead, he addressed himself to a rather esoteric issue in clergy politics that had arisen in the Diocesean Convention a short time before.

Ultimately this service ended, too.

It is hard for me to imagine a service, allegedly the worship of God, which would be a more vulgar travesty, though I suppose there are such services. In any case, my own humiliation for what this must have conveyed to my guest was now much more than it had been after the earlier service.

But it need not have been so. For afterwards he knew that what we had witnessed was neither the proclamation of

God's Word nor the worship of God, but something more like an alumni rite. And what was wrong with the preacher was not only that he did not bother with the Gospel, but that he also did not bother with the people of the congregation or with their lives and concerns and problems, whereas my guest knew that real preaching would be a kind of dialogue between the Word of God beheld in the Bible and the liturgy, on the one hand, and on the other the Word of God as it may be seen and heard within the common lives of the people of the congregation.

So my anxiety and wrath and shame were undone. My friend somehow understood something of the integrity of the Church in the Gospel in seeing and hearing an event which had little or none of that integrity. In other words, in every way, in truth but also in pretense, the Word of God is proclaimed.[2]

And this I relate in order to recall and to caution myself, as much as any other fond of protest, that as God's witness cannot be restricted or inhibited by falseness or weakness in the churches, neither must His witness await the return of the churches to a better unity and true faith.

At the same time, and with equal force, the freedom of God's own witness from the corruptions of the churches does not condone them, nor must that freedom be invoked as an excuse for squelching reformation. In fact the very vocation of the churches to become and be the Church is in order to honor and praise and participate in the witness of God to Himself in the world. The veracity and power of God's own witness is no answer to why the churches live so much as if they belonged to the world. It is God's own witness which warrants not only the accusations of the specific conformities and accommodations of the churches of Protestantism to the American ideas of religion, but also which enjoins hard attention to the organic life of the churches of Protestantism, to the office of the clergy and the ministry of the laity, the task of preaching, the work of prophetism,

2. Cf. Philippians 1:18.

the place of the seminary, the nature of the congregation, the meaning of the sacramental life, the problems of moral theology, the responsibility for apologetics, and the nature of evangelism.

One suspects that in American Protestantism, much of the confusion, not to mention error, about the nature of the Church and the respective ministries of the clergy and the laity has been incubated in the seminaries. At least the seminary is a decisive *locus* of these issues: they probably will not be resolved if they are not confronted in the seminary.

The ministry of the laity cannot mature until the priesthood is restored in the churches of American Protestantism.[3] What is more, both the renewal of the lay ministry and the restoration of the priesthood are unequivocally essential to any substantive ecumenical relationships of the Protestant churches with the other churches of Christendom.

But, alas, the contemporary Protestant seminary appears dilettantish about the ministry of the laity and recalcitrant in the preparation of a priesthood.

Or so it seems to me.

I am neither ordained nor seminarian: I am a layman. Yet I count that no disqualification to comment on the task of the seminary within the churches. Quite the contrary; it is, actually, the least self-serving credential for such comment. As other laymen, I observe the seminary mainly from the outside: its impact upon the congregation, its ramifications in the actual relations of clergy and laity, and its consequences for the images of the clergy and laity both in the common life of the churches and the public life of society. As it happens, too, I have also lectured in twenty-four seminaries of ten denominations and have participated in some conferences

3. I recognize that the use of the word "priesthood" may be provocative to some Protestants. It is used here in preference to "clergy" or "ministry" or "ordained ministry" to designate a particular office in the Church having responsibilities and functions distinguishable from the office and ministry of all baptised people, the laity. It is not used here as representing any specific denominational or institutional doctrine of the priesthood.

of the Interseminary Movement; to that extent, at least, my observation of the seminary has an empirical basis.

No Priesthood: No Laity

In the churches of Protestantism in America, much of the popularized discussion of the ministry of the laity has overlooked the radical interdependence and reciprocity between the functions of the priesthood and the laity in the total ministry of the Body of Christ in the world. There is no priesthood without a laity serving the world; there is no laity without a priesthood serving the laity. There is not one without the other. In many Protestant churches nowadays there is neither.

Wherever this prevails, the priesthood is abandoned or repudiated or so radically misconceived that the clergy have become a substitute laity whose function is to publicly represent — *in the place of the laity* — the presence of the Church in the world. The clergy have become hired spokesmen for religion among men. They have been invited to decorate public life, but restrained from intervening significantly in it. They have been relegated to the literal periphery — the invocations and the benedictions — of secular affairs. The clergy have become the face of the Church in the world; they have become a superficial, symbolic, ceremonial laity.

Such degrading of the ordained ministry is serious enough in itself, but it is commonly associated in the practical life of the churches with a laity who are mere spectators to religious exercises — paying their admission, as it were, to behold a pageant or cultus practice in which their critical and wholesome participation is neither expected not welcomed.

That the clergy act as a substitute laity and the laity are just observers of religion is, of course, consistent with and probably the product of the American idea that religion has only to do with religion, but not with the cares of the world.

The withdrawal of the churches from daily affairs and from the places in which men work and fight and play and rest and buy and sell is evident in a curious way even in those churches which remember and retain something of the integrity of the Church as the Body of Christ. For even in those churches with apparently great vitality and concern, the congregation has itself become the forum for evangelism — the place reserved for those who hope or want or wait to be evangelized. One rejoices wherever and whenever and however men are evangelized, but it is nonetheless an anomaly when the Church's evangelistic mission becomes internalized, when evangelization — rather than worship — becomes characteristic of the interior life of a congregation. The world and the ordinary places in the world are the evangelistic precincts for Christians, whereas the congregation is the singular gathering of those who *are* evangelized for the public celebration of the Word of God, namely, worship. Where the congregation, instead of the marketplace, becomes the *locus* of evangelism, both the world and worship are lucky to have lip service. Moreover, the relations of clergy and laity then become ambiguous and confused and touchy because it is easily and secretly assumed by both clergy and laity that the clergy are the company of the evangelized and the laity are heathen. Evangelistic effort is not apt to be authenticated in such circumstances, worship is bound to be inhibited, and, meanwhile, the world outside is forgotten.

Sometimes this compounded frustration of the Church's given life of worship, evangelism, and care for the world, with its accompanying insecurities for both clergy and laity, is rationalized by permitting some laymen to become *quasi*-clergy, by enlisting them in the tasks of preserving and protecting and administering the ecclesiastical entity of the congregation. To be a layman then means to be a Sunday School teacher or an usher or a fund-raiser or a doner or a vestryman or a club member or a Scoutmaster or a member of the choir or a parson's handyman. These churchly and churchy activities I do not — necessarily — deprecate, save when such appurtenances so clutter the life of a congregation that its vocation of worship is obscured or forsaken, or where such activities keep the laity confined to the premises of the congregation and discourage the laity from dispersing into the world, or where the office of the Christian is trivially defined in such works.

But the most subtle and beguiling separation imposed in the churches between the participation of the laity in the internal life of the congregation and their participation in the common life of the world is that which supposes that religion has somehow to at last be made relevant to the decisional predicaments of daily work or family life or politics or what not. This well-intentioned, exceedingly popular, and very pernicious doctrine asserts that the content and relationships of religion are strangely different from the content and relationships of secular life, and that, therefore, some application of the propositions of religion is required to make them relevant to secular issues. The things of God are remote from the things of men, though sufficiently pious men may connect the two. This attitude is reminiscent of Greek religion — and it ingeniously survives today in theosophy and Zen and, in a sallow and arrogant form, in Moral Re-Armament — but it has no echo in the Gospel of Jesus Christ.

In Jesus Christ there is no chasm between God and the world.

Jesus Christ means that God cares extremely, decisively, inclusively, immediately for the ordinary, transient, proud, wonderful, besetting, profane, frivolous, heroic, lusty things of men. The reconciliation of God and the world in Jesus Christ means that in Christ there is a radical and integral relationship of all men and of all things. *In Him all things are held together.*[4]

The Church as the Body of Christ in the world has, shares, manifests, and represents that same radical integrity. All who are in Christ — each member of His Body in the world — know and live in the same integrity in his relationships with any creature in his own, specific personal history. Existentially and empirically, the reconciliation of the world with God in Jesus Christ establishes a man in unity with both God and the whole world. The singular life of the Christian is

4. Colossians 1:17b.

a sacrament — a recall, a representation, an enactment, a communication — of that given actual unity, whether in the gathering of the worshipping congregation now and then or whether in the scattering of the members within the daily affairs of the world. To put it mildly, then, it is careless and misleading to speak of the action of God in the world in Christ in terms of "making the Gospel relevant" to the secular. The Body of Christ lives in the world in the unity between God and the world wrought in Christ and, in a sense, the Body of Christ lives in the world *as* the unity of God and the world in Christ.

The Body of Christ lives in the world on behalf of the world, in intercession for the world. In the most esoteric and, even to many clergy and church people, apparently remote and irrelevant image of that life, when a congregation gathers in sacramental worship, the members of the Body are offering the world to God, not for His sake, not for their own sake, but for the sake of the world, and the members then and there celebrate God's presence in the world, and on behalf of the world, even though that world does not yet discern His presence. So, too, in the most frequent and ordinary image of that life, in the secret action of some Christian in the marketplace, God's presence there is discerned and exposed on behalf of the world, and that place and those who may be in that place are consecrated to God, for their own sake — that is, because of their unbelief. The vocation of each member of the Body is participation in that intercession in every such experience, wherever and whenever it occurs.

It is this congruence in the Christian life in the whole Church and in the life of each member of the Church that so offends the world. The confidence of the Christian task is that there is nowhere an escape from the Word of God.[5] The joy of the Christian life is that nowhere is the Word of God absent. The audacity of the Christian way is in acknowl-

5. Cf. Psalm 139:7.

edging the Word of God in all things and in all men and in every place and at any time on behalf of the world — yes, even a world which really does not acknowledge Him or worship Him in any thing, or in any man, or in any time or place. To the world — especially, I suppose, in an ostensibly self-sufficing, pseudo-religious, generically pietistic society like the United States — this is scandalous intolerance. But to the Christian it is patient fear of the Living God.

The Service of the Priesthood to the Laity

The cohesion and commonalty of the vocation of Christians originates in their power to discern the truth of the Word of God in any event whatever, and precisely because the Word of God is present in all events, that power may be exercised in any event. The practice of the intensely singular vocation of Christians is manifold and extraordinarily versatile. There are many parts to the one Body which is Christ's.[6] No man — for that matter, no creature, no idea, no institution, no nation, no issue, no action — is beyond the reach and intercession of some member of the Body of Christ. It is in this way, indeed, that is, by the width and the depth of the implication of Christians in the life of the world, that the unequivocal fact of grace is communicated, that the universality of Christ is represented, and that the ubiquity of the Word of God in the world is exposed.

For lay folk in the Church this means that there is no forbidden work. There is no corner of human existence, however degraded or neglected, into which they may not venture; no person, however beleaguered or possessed, whom they may not befriend and represent; no cause, however vain or stupid, in which they may not witness; no risk, however costly or imprudent, which they may not undertake.

This intimacy with the world as it is, this peculiar freedom, this awful innocence toward the world which a Christian is given, makes a Christian look like a sucker. He looks like that to other men because he is engaged in the wholesale ex-

6. Cf. Romans 3:9-12, and Psalm 14:1-2, 53:1-2.

penditure of his life. He looks like that because he is without caution or prudence in preserving his own life. He looks like that because he is not threatened by the power of death either over his own life or over the rest of the world. He looks like that because he is free to give his life — to die — imminently, today, for the sake of any one or anything at all, even for those or that which seem unworthy of his death, thereby celebrating the One who died for all though none be worthy, not even one.[7]

A Christian is not distinguished by his political views, or moral decisions, or habitual conduct, or personal piety, or, least of all, by his churchly activities. A Christian is distinguished by his radical esteem for the Incarnation — to use the traditional jargon — by his reverence for the life of God in the whole of Creation, even and, in a sense, especially, Creation in the travail of sin.

The characteristic place to find a Christian is among his very enemies.

The first place to look for Christ is in Hell.

For those ordained by the Church for the priesthood, this means that their office and ministry are located at the interstices of the Body of Christ and of the congregations which represent that Body visibly and notoriously in the world. The ministry of the priesthood is a ministry to the members of the Body in their relations to each other, relations consequent to their incredibly diversified ministry within the world. The ministry of the priesthood is one directed to the most sophisticated life of the Church, the Church, that is, gathered as a congregation in worship, assembled for the exposition and exhibition of the Word of God. This is the ministry addressed to the care and nurture of the members of the Body of Christ for the sake of their several, various, and common uses in the world. This is the ministry serving those people who come out of the world now and then to worship God together and encompass and include in their intercessions to Him the cares of all the world as they know it and are

7. Cf. I Corinthians 12:19.

involved in it. This is the ministry of confession in which the task and witness of each member of the Body is heard and related to that of all other members of the Body who are now or who have ever been or, indeed, who are yet to be. This is the ministry which cares for and conserves the tradition of the Church — that is, the continuity and integrity of the Christian mission ever since Pentecost. This is the ministry devoted to the health and holiness of the Body of Christ in the world.

This is a glorious, jubilant, crucial, humble ministry, but this is a ministry nowadays largely abandoned in Protestantism and for which, evidently, precious little preparation is made in the seminaries of Protestantism.

Candidates for seminary admission in Protestantism have not, very often, in the first instance, been invited into such a ministry. They have instead been invited into a community of students and scholars examining the history of religion. Or they have been recruited as those who would devote some time, perhaps their working lives, to inquiry into the religious situation. Or they have been induced to think of the ordained ministry as a profession and specialty, like social work or medicine or law.[8] They are expected only, though sometimes necessarily, to have an academic interest in the Christian faith. And there has been much emphasis upon the amenities of the "profession of the ministry," that is, clergy salaries and pensions and household allowances and long vacations and social status and the like.[9]

Some seminarians think and some seminary faculty assume that ordination, *rather than baptism,* is the seal of the Christian life — providing for those who have it the assurance and security that they are indeed Christians. That leads, nowadays, as it did in the days preceding the Reformation, to a stylized clericalism within the Church, to the segregation of

8. This has been the line in some efforts sponsored by the National Council of Churches to recruit candidates for the ordained ministry from among high school students.

9. *Ibid.*

clergy from the laity, to the assumption by the clergy of the tasks of the laity, and to the inevitable neglect of the tasks of both clergy and laity.

Related to this attitude, and to the professionalization of the clergy, at least in American society, is the treatment of theology as an academic discipline within the seminaries. The notion seems to be that theology is comparable in its content and methodology to the disciplines — law or mathematics or political science — of the university. But this overweighs the similarities between theology and the academic disciplines and overlooks the essential fact that theology — historical or pastoral or systematic or moral — is always in the first instance confessional. The very articulation and communication of the theological meaning of human experience and of the affairs of the world is primarily a confessional act and event — that is, an immediate and contemporary confession of the presence of the life of God in the world and a declaration and interpretation of His life in the world. To put it another way, theology is qualitatively different from the academic disciplines because it is never an abstract, theoretical, or just historical exercise, but rather an examination of the actual data of the world's existence in the faith that the Word of God is evident in that data and may be identified, discussed, studied, verified, imparted, and enjoyed. Theology is not — unlike philosophy or physics or geography — a merely human science and endeavor. The academic sciences are concerned with the knowledge of man, of mankind, and the world and the relationships between mankind and the world. Theology is about the knowledge God gives men of Himself in and through the life of mankind and the world's existence.

The imitation in theology of the academic disciplines is, therefore, a particularly perilous practice; it tends to disclaim and discount the present activity and continuing initiative of God in the world. Academic theology degenerates into religious philosophy, and religious philosophy is constructed on the premise that God is not a living power and presence but a convenient speculative proposition. Theology is a confessional event; religious philosophy is an esoteric idolatry.[10]

The conformity of theology to the academic categories, as it is presented and represented all too often in the seminaries, has meant the gradual but increasing fascination and identification of the seminary with the university and the consequent separation of the seminary from the Church. The seminaries — especially the so-called interdenominational or non-denominational institutions — become centers of religious studies, attracting those interested in inquiries into religious experience and history. That is a very commendable thing, to my mind, and probably any real university needs such a center, alongside the business school and the medical school and the law school and the graduate divisions in the humanities, arts and sciences, but such a school is not apt to supply a priesthood for the Church. Indeed, in one university-affiliated seminary at the present time, over 70 percent of the enrolled students indicate that they are not intending to present themselves for the parish ministry. They will, instead, be teachers and social workers and agency executives and ecumenical staff and ecclesiastical bureaucrats. Even among those eventually ordained from such seminaries, the danger is that they will come to regard the ordained ministry as a profession pertaining to a certain commodity — religion — which they have been trained in their particular trade school to manufacture or procure and market. Appropriately, now, for such candidates for the ordained ministry there is even a test for seminary admission designed to project and predict the aptitude of a given applicant for this profession and for its training schools.[11]

Another danger, of course, in the drifting of the seminary away from the Church, in the academicizing of theology, and in the professionalizing of the ordained ministry, is the vested interest which seminary faculty, seminarians, and seminary graduates acquire in theology as their specialty and proficiency. One would think that theology is an origination of

10. See Colossians 2:8-19.
11. This test was designed by the Educational Testing Service at Princeton for experimental use by several major denominations.

seminary professors and a possession of only those who are seminary-instructed. One would think that the work of theology is the province and responsibility only of the ordained ministry. Yet the work of theology is a work of the whole people of God — laity as well as clergy, and even though many laity may be just as glad to have the clergy assume responsibility in theology, that does not change the fact that some aspects of theology — that is, specifically the work of apologetics and moral theology — are peculiarly the office of the laity in the encounter in their practical lives between the Word of God and the ordinary life of the world.

Nevertheless, the idea is deeply embedded in American Protestantism that the clergy go to seminary in order to become theologians. I recall, for example, giving a lecture at a seminary a while ago in which I made a remark which particularly agitated the Dean of the seminary, and he said to me, "No responsible theologian would say what you just said!" That seemed to me reassuring news. A few days later I received a letter from someone who had been present at this exchange. The letter declared that the Dean had been mistaken and that in fact Soren Kierkegaard had written in his journals somewhere the substance of what I had said. I reported this comforting and distinguished citation to the Dean, who without hesitation announced: "Oh, Kierkegaard is not a responsible theologian." How could he be? He was no seminary professor. How could he know much about the mystery of God's presence in the world? Kierkegaard, after all, was only in the world — where God is — not in the seminary — where the theologians are!

Moreover, even at the self-styled frontiers of American Protestantism, where there is concern for the participation of the laity in the theological work of the Church, the institutes and communities and academies organized for lay people bear much resemblance to the seminary, especially in the tendency within them to treat theology abstractly and academically.

Unhappily enough, many clergymen and seminarians, for all their apparent sophistication in academic theology, often

are shockingly ignorant of the Bible. Perhaps they are taught
a lot about the Bible, but they know far too little of the Bible.
Or so it appears, since they so seldom rely upon the Bible in
preaching. Instead of the exposition of the Word of God
in the Bible in preaching, laymen are subjected to all manner
of speeches, diatribes, commentaries, newscasts, patriotic de-
clamations, poetic recitations, aphorisms, positive thoughts,
social analysis, gimmicks, solicitations, sentimentalities, and
corn.

The unBiblical tenor of much Protestant preaching is
strange, of course, in Protestantism because the opening of
the Bible within the congregation was one of the historic
promises of the Reformation. It seems in America to have
been forgotten. If the Bible were to be again restored to
centrality in preaching within the congregation, it might also
be realized that preaching is a very common and self-effacing
work of the ordained ministry. Preaching is not, after all, a
charismatic gift of the Holy Spirit, but an ordinary characteristic of the gathered life of a congregation. Preaching is the
faithful, historically responsive, enthusiastic utterance of the
Word of God in order that the Word of God may be beheld, heard, and enjoyed by those who are witnesses to the
preaching. Preaching is the celebration of the Word of God
within the Church for the sake of the world, and preaching,
therefore, always bespeaks the modesty of the Church, or
of a particular congregation of the Church, as the representative of the world before God. Preaching *never* boasts
of the Church, preaching *never* commends the Church to
men, preaching *never* argues or tries to prove or convince
or persuade anybody. Preaching only flaunts and displays
the content, grandeur, simplicity, integrity and power of the
Word of God in the world as it is evidenced in the Bible and
in the world's contemporary life. Preaching is integral to
that work of the Church called worship — the remembrance,
recital, enactment, obedience to, exposure of the Word of
God, the thanksgiving and anticipation for the Word of
God, and the unhesitant, reckless excitement in the presence
of the Word of God in history.

It takes a servant of the Word of God to be a preacher. It takes a humble man to be a preacher. It takes a sinner to be a preacher. It takes courage and humor and love to be a preacher. It takes a real priest to be a preacher in the congregation. It takes one who is so familiar with and so fond of the Word of God in the Bible that he will put forth the Word in his preaching without gratuitous embellishments, without appending his latest interesting opinions, and without commending himself or his personality, but merely commending the Word of God to the people whom he serves.

The neglect of the Bible in Protestant preaching is the more serious in those churches, which are legion, which do not have or use a liturgy which is itself wrought from Scripture. At least, where there is a Scriptural liturgy, the people are assured that the Word of God will be addressed and represented to them when they gather as a congregation, even if the sermon does not happen to be a proclamation and illumination of God's Word. In much of Protestantism there is no such assurance that the content of the public service will be worship, that is, will be the radical utterance of the Word of God among His people and their discernment and acknowledgement and thanksgiving for His Word.

Where the preaching and liturgical offices of the priesthood have been neglected or forsaken, the confessional life of the congregation is invariably empty. Since the earliest communities of Christians, confession of sin, which is always at the same time confession of the faith — of the saving power of God in Christ — has been a public characteristic of the congregation.[12] It is here that the priest stands in the midst of the Body, hearing the confession of each member as the representative of all the members in the assurance of God's forgiveness and in the acceptance of all the members of the Body of each other. This is not a private or unilateral relationship between a man and God, much less between a layman and a priest, but, on the contrary, represents the most daring and intimate practice of the corporate Christian life,

12. Cf. James 5:13-16.

necessarily implicating each member of the Body in care and
intercession for the rest, and of the whole Body for each
member. This is, too, in a sense, the most explicitly eschato-
logical action within a congregation, anticipating the Last
Day when God's judgment for all men is publicized and
when no secret can any more be hidden by any man; indeed,
this is a way of calling for that Day to come. This is no
formalistic or perfunctory incident to the life of the congregation, but indispensable to the very possibility and reality
and honesty of public worship. It is actually the beginning
of worship. And it is the substance of and enablement of
pastoral care.

Yet confession hardly survives in contemporary Protestantism. Improvisations have been introduced more or less
in the place of confession, some of them concocted in the
seminaries which each year discharge men for the ordained
ministry who are amateur, part-time therapists or who have
been enough indoctrinated in group dynamics to fancy their
skill in human manipulation, or who earnestly intend to
"work with people in solving their problems." No discount
is made here for the significance of psychiatry and psychology,
but these skills will not be acquired in the seminaries. And no
one who has been in politics, as I have, would minimize the
importance of what is lately called "group dynamics," but
neither is this a substitute in the Church for confession and
absolution and intercession. And social work, as professional-
ly immature as it is, is a necessary discipline in urban society,
but the priesthood, and nothing less than or other than that,
is essential in every congregation.

Let the seminaries and the seminarians be mindful of the
world about them, but let nothing distract either seminary or
seminarian from the preparation of a priesthood and, indeed,
from the restoration of a priesthood to Protestantism.

The Service of the Laity to the World

What has been happening in the seminaries of Protestantism,
at least as it looks from outside the seminaries, that is, from

within the congregation, or in the relationships of clergy and laity in the churches and in society, is the preparation, not of a priesthood, but of a moderately literate and informed laity. But if a seminary graduate is really that, if that's what he wants to be and is prepared to be, what happens when he is ordained and takes a job as a clergyman? If in his work he is placed in contact with laymen who are not mere nominal Christians, there is apt to be difficulty, for he will often be engaged in what they understand to be their proper ministry and service to the world.

One Bishop, within whose Diocese there are numbers of alert and articulate and practicing Christians, complains that his chief problem is that "my laymen threaten the devil out of my clergy."

Such tension may arise in a congregation where the laity are disinclined to be spectators or to do errands within the parish, but look to the gathered community as the place and event to which they constantly return from their witness in the daily life of the world to share the cares and rejoicing of their vocation with the other members of this Body in the trust and celebration of the Gospel, that is, worship. Such issues may arise in a congregation where it is known that the total ministry of Christ's Body includes both priesthood and laity, whose functions, though different, are incomplete without each other and cannot be substituted one for the other.

Reference has already been made to the contradictions which are present when the congregation, rather than the marketplace, becomes the place of evangelism, to the debilitating effect of the abandonment of Biblical preaching and a Biblical liturgy in the congregation upon the service and support of the ministry of the laity in the world, and to the significance of confession in the public life and pastoral care of the congregation. But here it should be noticed that among the tasks which belong essentially to the laity in their service in and to the world there are some which now are commonly thought of as prerogatives of the ordained ministry. In Protestantism this is particularly the case with the prophetic ministry of the Church. Even while the preachers of Protestantism have relied with diminishing interest upon the Bible in their preaching, they have often associated the work of preaching with the work of prophetism. Yet there is no association in principle or historically or functionally between the priest and preacher on the one hand and the prophet on the other. On the contrary, the former's task is the responsible utterance of the Word of God within the congregation — so that the Word may be acknowledged and admired there, and so that those who gather as the congregation may be identified by the Word of God in their corporate life as the Body of Christ, and so that they may be so enlightened by the Word of God within the congregation that they will become sensitive to and perceptive of the Word of God as they encounter the Word in the common life of the world in which their various ministries as lay people take place. But it is out in the world, not within the congregation, that the prophetic task is exercised. The prophet is characteristically not priest and preacher, but layman. His task is to represent and expose the Word of God in the world, and particularly in the posture of the Word which stands over against the world's existence and the world's disregard of and arrogance toward the Word of God. And sometimes his task is to declare and convey the Word of God as it stands over against the worldliness of the Church. In either instance, prophetism is not located within the congregation, nor is prophetism peculiarly associated with preaching in the congregation; rather, prophetism is identified with the clash between the existence of the world and the presence of the Word of God in the world and, as well, with the tension between the life of the Church at any given point and the Word of God whose presence in the world the Church exists to hear, herald and expose.

While the work of prophetism is characteristically associated with the laity rather than the priesthood, it is nevertheless true that where a congregation is a confessing community, and where, within a congregation, there is reliance upon the Word of God in the Bible in preaching and in sacramental life, the very existence of such a congregation has a prophetic impact upon the secular life which surrounds it. For then the congregation represents to the world the life to which the world is called; then the life of the congregation prophesies the world which is to come in God's patience, judgment and mercy.

Much the same thing as has been said about the laity's prophetic ministry to the world can be said about the other aspects of the service of the laity to the world. Apologetics — the defense and explication of the Gospel against the world's hostility to the Word of God — accompanies the ordinary involvement of the laity in daily work and politics and business and culture. No Christian can get by for very long in any kind of secular work or profession or activity without encountering the misconceptions which the world has about the Gospel, and without being exposed to the enmity which the world bears toward the Gospel. To be silent in the face of such perversion of the faith or of such aggression against the faith is to become an accomplice. The laity cannot be saved from the apologetic task associated with their participation in the practical affairs of the world by the pronouncements of ecclesiastical authorities nor by the ministry of the clergy. Each layman must be his own apologist, responsible for his stewardship of the Gospel in his daily life and work.

Part of the stewardship goes beyond apologetics — beyond defense of the Gospel in the marketplace — and takes up the work of moral theology, that is, the interpretation and articulation, from time to time, of the significance of the Word of God in social conflict and change. It is in this area that much confusion exists in the churches as to the mutual roles of clergy and laity. Most of the churches' departments of social education and action are served by clergy in circumstances which require the clergy to abstain from exercising the priestly functions for which, hopefully, they are ordained. And, at the same time, these programs seek to involve large numbers of lay people in the name of the mission of the Church in the world, whereas in fact such programs divert laymen from the mission in the world, that is, from a full involvement in secular affairs because of the attrition resulting from participation in churchly activity and discussion about secular affairs. The Christian social witness is achieved only insofar as Christians are deeply implicated in the real life of society — in unions and political clubs and citizen groups and the like; it is not made by Christian people gathering off by themselves in a parish house to study and discuss social issues. Witness becomes possible only when the Christian is on the actual scene where the conflict is taking place, the decision is being made, the legislation is being enacted.

Remember, though, that the witness made in the forums of public life is apt to be a secret witness, and not one which becomes known or openly recognized as Christian witness. It more and more appears to me that the Christian witness is exhibited dramatically in the world mainly when the congregation assembles for public worship. But when the members of the Body disperse into and within the common life of the world, the Christian witness is secret, known only to those actually involved in and reached by the witness being made, known only in the event itself, except as it becomes known to other Christians in the particular intercessions of the Church for the world around.

And part of the stewardship of the Gospel by the laity in the world is intentionally, necessarily, and candidly evangelistic. It is the market place, as has been pointed out, not the congregation or the premises of the Church, which is the place of evangelism. It is a work which cannot be done with fanfare — lest the uniqueness with which the Gospel addresses each man in his own life be vitiated. Nor is there some stereotyped scheme of evangelization. Evangelism is not essentially verbal, even though it seems commonly to be believed that the recitation of certain words constitute efficacious evangelism. Evangelism consists of loving another human being in a way which represents to him the care of God for his particular life. Evangelism rests upon the appeal to another man to remember his own creation — to remember Who made him and for Whom he was made. Evangelism is the event in which a Christian confronts another man in a way which assures the other man that the new life which he observes in the Christian is vouchsafed for him also.

The care which the Christian has for the world, the service of the laity to the world, is constituted in the very knowledge which is unveiled and praised in sacramental worship and preaching in the congregation: the Word of God is here and now among us in the world. The Christian life is a reliance upon that knowledge, a reliance lived among men, amidst all the powers and authorities in the world, in all things, in every place, at any time, in a way which discloses the presence of the Word of God to those who have not yet discerned Him and in a way which affirms and loves that Truth about those who do not yet know Him.

The Simplicity of the Christian Life

And whatever you do, in word or deed, do everything in the name of the Lord Jesus, giving thanks to God the Father through him.

Colossians 3:17

THE SIMPLICITY — not ease — but simplicity of the Christian life is founded upon the fact of the presence of the Word of God already in the common life of the world. The practice of the Christian life consists of the discernment of (the seeing and hearing), and the reliance upon (the reckless and uncalculating dependence), and the celebration (the ready and spontaneous enjoyment) of the presence of the Word of God in the common life of the world.

The world to which Christians refer when they speak of the presence of the Word of God in the world is *this* world. It is the same world in which you and I live. It is not a make-believe world: not some non-existent or not yet existent world, not some world of aspiration or anticipation, not some imagined or imaginary world, not some world after this world, but this world. It is the world in which you and I and other men live and talk and laugh and buy and sell and lust and love and fight and die. It is the world that you or I or any man apprehends and knows in all the ordinary ways — the world we touch and smell and hear and see. It is *this* world, the world we know, this world just as it is into which God comes, for which God cares, in which God is with us, in which the Word of God resides.

The Word of God is present and evident not only in the world which seems to you or to me or to somebody else good or true or clean or beautiful, but, to those who are not blind, the Word of God is also present and evident in the world which seems to you or me or another evil or false or filthy or ugly. So it is that in all events, in every circumstance, and, at last, even in the face of death, God is here and may be known.

It is to be noted that God is not especially or exclusively present in the Church. His presence is in the world. The Church exists only as that community in the world which cares about, observes, and testifies about God's presence in the world in all things, at every time and place. The Church is only the company of those who know of and rejoice in the presence of God in the world. But it is not first of all the Church which has introduced God to the world. God knows the world, and, indeed, the world is His own, without the Church. The Church has only the task of introducing the world to God, that is, exposing through her discernment of and reliance on and celebration of the presence of the Word of God in the world, the world to God. It is, after all, a plain and simple task which is given to the Church.

The experience of being a Christian is one of continually encountering in the ordinary and everyday events of life the same Word of God which is announced and heard, remembered and dramatized, expected and fulfilled in the sanctuary of the Church. To celebrate the Word of God in the sacramental worship of a congregation is an anticipation of the discernment of the same Word of God in the common life of the world. To be in the presence of the Word of God while in the world authenticates the practice of sacramental life within the congregation. One confirms and is confirmed by the other. In each place, in both world and Church, the Word is the same Word, and, in each place, in both practical life and sacramental life, the response elicited and the task required of the Christian is the same.

It is this experience which marks the Christian. It is this integrity of life, and, indeed, of his very being, this interpenetration of his secular and religious lives which identifies the Christian. It is this, and not the externals which are sometimes vehemently asserted as marks of the Christian life — like dress or diet or personal morality or what not. And part of the strength and power of the Christian life is realism. Christians know that the Word of God, which they celebrate as the Church, is present already in this world, in this world as it is, not as one might wish it to be. So Christians do not blush or flinch or equivocate or ignore or hide from or deny or try to disguise anything about this world as it is. Christians know that there is darkness as well as light. Christians know there is war and disease and poverty and pain and lust and hate as well as peace and health and security and comfort and love and forgiveness. There is no extremity of human experience unknown to a Christian or which he must fear or deny.

My own ordinary life in the world has been in the past several years as a practicing attorney. For five of those years, my work was mainly in the East Harlem neighborhood in New York City. Something of what I know of the presence of the Word of God in the life of the world I know from living and working in East Harlem. But before mentioning anything about that, a word of caution: East Harlem is perhaps the most notorious slum in New York City, and the physical appearance of the neighborhood is very different from, say, Northampton, Massachusetts, where I was raised, or from Cambridge, Massachusetts where I studied law, or from the communities familiar to most American Protestants. In what follows I do not propose to tell horror stories about the slums — although that would be easy to do — because that would not be very edifying in itself, and might just be a morbid entertainment, and, anyway, it would be an exploitation of the people who live in this neighborhood, people already enough exploited in one way or another.

No one, moreover, should be misled into thinking that because the empirical difference between an East Harlem and a Northampton are very obvious, this means that there are also essential differences between the two. The issue of life is, in all significant respects, the same in one place as in the other. That is to say, the presence and action of God in the world is astonishingly consistent and self-consistent, and He has not forsaken any sector of the world, nor any man.

Or, to put it a bit differently, I know nothing about God

in a speculative or hypothetical sense, and I am able to speak
of Him only out of my own experience of His presence, on
the one hand, in the common life of the world as I participate
in it, and, on the other hand, the life of the Church as I
participate in that.

The Presence of the Word of God in the World

West Side Story was a highly popular and successful musical
play and now is a similarly well-received motion picture. (I
would think that it could also be used shrewdly as a document for discussion in Sunday Schools, in place of some of
the ridiculous curriculum materials now in use.) *West Side
Story* is a musical and a movie, but it is also many other
things, and all of them at the same time. First of all, it is
a business venture. Some people invested money in this
property, hoping for a profit. *West Side Story* is commerce.
But *West Side Story* is also literature — it is an attempt to
retell, in a contemporary idiom, the story of Romeo and
Juliet. *West Side Story* is music. While I know very little
about music, it appears to me that it is good music. *West
Side Story* is also a social document. It is sociology. I do
know something about that. *West Side Story*, in, for example,
the song *Gee, Officer Krupke!*, is a more accurate presentation and insight into how the kids in the gangs in New
York City feel toward the police and the courts and the social
workers and the psychiatrists and their parents and the places
where they live than almost any other social document that
presently exists. Anyway, *West Side Story* is a social document, and I would consider it a penetrating and important
one. But *West Side Story* is also theology, and it is theology
while it remains theater and motion picture, a business enterprise, literature, music, sociology. It is theology while it
remains all of the other things which it is, and without vio-
lating the integrity of any of the other things which it is. In
fact, these other things are the vehicles through which *West
Side Story* as theology is conveyed.

What happens in *West Side Story?* Two gangs, one
Puerto Rican, the other Italian, are deeply estranged. They

are enemies. They fight. A boy is killed. And out of the death of the boy, the gangs are reconciled. Does that sound familiar? It is familiar if you have ever opened and listened to the Bible. It is familiar if you have ever heard and beheld the Gospel in the Church. *One dies and many are reconciled. That* is the Word of God. And here it is a Word hidden within all the words and action of the play and motion picture, and within all the other things which *West Side Story* is in its common appearance — that is, as literature and music, commerce and sociology and so on.

West Side Story commends itself as an example of how the Word of God is present in the common life of the world in part because it is now so widely familiar, but also for another reason, which is that, in a curious way, *West Side Story* really happened:

Some summers ago, in New York, there were all together eleven homicides as a result of gang warfare in the city. One of the killings (as I recall, it was the second of the summer) happened in the East Harlem neighborhood. Two gangs — one Italian, one Puerto Rican — were engaged in skirmishes over the respective territories that each would occupy for the summer. One of the issues at stake was which gang would have jurisdiction over and use of a public swimming pool in the neighborhood. The skirmishes were a part, of course, of a larger warfare precipitated by the Puerto Rican migration to the city and by the necessity for Puerto Rican boys to fight for some space in which to live and by the resistance of those already in the neighborhood to these newcomers. In the fight between these two particular gangs, in the fight over the pool, a boy was killed. The boy who was killed happened to be the brother of the war counsellor of one of the gangs. In gang society, the war counsellor is the governor of the gang — the one who makes policy, the leader. He is not always the strongest or toughest boy in the gang, but he is commonly the smartest and most courageous. Unlike adult politics, when these kids choose a leader, they choose the one who has brains and guts. In any case, the boy who died was the brother of such a war counsellor.

On the night of the fight, on the night of the death, the brother of the boy who had been killed spent a long time alone, mourning his brother and brooding about his death and the meaning of this death. And then he went from his mourning to his counterpart in the other gang, to the war counsellor of the other gang, to his mortal enemy, to the one whose gang had killed his brother. He went alone. He went without weapons or bodyguards or tricks. He went alone — without advice from anybody — clergy or lawyers or social workers or police or the Youth Board or anybody else. He went alone to his enemy — and they talked of what had happened, they talked about this death and what it meant for those still living. And then these two boys went to leaders of several other gangs in that immediate section of East Harlem. And, after awhile, a council was formed to discuss and negotiate the differences amongst the gangs involved. Some very radical things have come from this. For one thing, there has been no serious physical violence — and no homicides involving boys from these gangs — since the council was formed. Another is that they even invited a cop — the precinct captain — to sit down with them and say whatever he wanted to say and hear what they had to say. That's probably the first time in the history of these kids and these cops that they have confronted each other in any situation except one of radical hostility and suspicion. Well, it is the same story: *one died and many are reconciled* — and many more are still being reconciled.

The Word of God — the same Word uttered and observed in the sanctuary — is hidden in the ordinary life of these boys in gang society and in the violence of the streets which is part of their everyday existence. And so it is within the common life of all the world.

The simplicity of the Christian life is this, that Christians are free to live within the common life of the world, to live in the assurance and excitement of knowing that they live in the presence of God's Word, no matter where, no matter what. Christians live in the enjoyment of the Word of God in the world for the sake of exposing the Word to others.

This is the only service which Christians owe the world, and all else they do or may do, including what they do in their sanctuaries, is encompassed in this service.

The Power to Discern the Word of God

Though the Word of God dwells in the world and is present within the common life of the world, not every man by any means knows or acknowledges that presence in history and in his own action and experience. Though the Word of God may be discerned in the passion and conflict of East Harlem gang society, for instance, that is no warrant that the very people within whose words and action the Word of God is hidden will see or hear the Word, will understand the theological meaning of their own lives, will care about the knowledge of God given to them in and through their own concrete and everyday existence. And if a man cannot see and sense the Word of God within his own history, he will not have the eyes to see or the sense to realize the presence of the Word in the larger history of the world or in the lives of other men or of nations, much less see any importance or relevance to the Church and the peculiar life of the Church in proclamation and celebration of the presence of the Word of God in the common life of the world.

The power to discern the Word of God is the mark of the Christian. It is not just one of an assortment of marks of the Christian; it is, in a sense, the unique mark essential to everything else which generally characterizes the Christian life. There can be no witness in the world to the Word of God by Christians individually or as the Church, save by the exercise of this power. There can be, of course, some witness to the Church, or to the churches, but neither of these is the same as the witness of Christians to the Word of God.

God witnesses to Himself in history whether or not there are Christians engaged in any witness to Him. The possibility of the witness of Christians as the Body of Christ and as members of the Body of Christ to the Word of God in the world depends upon the power given to Christians to discern the presence of the Word in the world. Further, and in the same fashion, there can be no worship, unless the power to discern the Word of God in the world is present. For how shall men worship that which they do not know? What is there to declare and present and celebrate, if the Word of God is not continually discovered and exposed in the life of the world? That which is called worship that is not consequent to the power to discern the Word of God in the world is not worship in a Biblical and Christian sense, but some superstitious practice, some foolish religiosity, some obscene idolatry.

The event of witness and the possibility of worship both originate in the power given to Christians to discern the presence of the Word of God in the world's common life.

Now if God's Word is present in common life, even though hidden except to the apprehension of faith, then the Word of God itself constitutes the essential and radical truth of common life and of every and any aspect of the world's existence at any and all times. It is in the Word of God that the secret of life is to be known. It is the Word of God that surpasses the dominion of death over the world's existence. The power, then, to discern the presence of the Word of God in the saga of the world's existence, reckoning with even the most puny human life, is a saving knowledge. The power to discern the presence of the Word of God in common life is the gift of life itself, the restoration of life, the beginning of new life. The power to discern the presence of the Word of God in the world is the knowledge of the Resurrection.

I have found that my own anxieties always contain the knowledge, the triumph and the enjoyment of God.

He descended into Hell.

That is very cheerful news.

There is nothing less than Hell unknown to Him. There is nothing that I have known this side of Hell that is unfamiliar to Him. There is nothing known to me which I am wont to call Hell which He has not already known. Nor is there anything beyond these realms which, even though unknown to me, He does not know.

Anxieties, therefore, are not unwelcome in my life or in my household, since anxieties do not end in themselves, as the psychiatrists assert.

Now, unlike the existentialists, I have no particular fondness for despair or loneliness or indifference or lust or boredom or the similar anxieties. But they beguile me no more. Nor do I any more fear them — either for the attraction and terror they own in themselves, or for that dreadful power of which they are the foretaste: *death*.

Anxieties do not end in death.

Anxieties end in God.

Anxieties are both overcome and completed in Christ. Christ is both the end and fulfillment of all anxieties.

Christ means, after all, simply that God is radically intimate with human history and experience in all its grandeur and diversity and personality. Christ has already lived my life. Christ has already died my death. Christ is risen from death for me.

And for any man at all.

The event of becoming a Christian is that event in which a man confronts and confesses the presence and power of death in his own life — in every facet and detail of his own personality, in every fact and experience of his own biography, in recollection of every word he has ever uttered and of every one he has ever known, and of every thing he has ever done while in the same event he is exposed to and beholds the power and presence of God which is greater than death. In that event he is given the power to discern God's presence in the world.

By that event in my own history I am sure — as sure as I am of my own being and biography — that no man confronts and struggles with and surrenders to any of the powers of death — any anxieties — any crisis — without beholding the power and the truth of the Resurrection: the presence of God in history which is greater than any of death's threats or temptations and more potent and which endures forever.

Now I am sure of the Resurrection.

In this way, by the demonstration of the presence of God confronted in my own dying, I become a witness to the timeliness, excitement, veracity, scope and grace of the Resurrection. It is not just some long ago event. It is at once long ago and here and now. It is no myth. It is no mere imaginative interpretation of the Truth: it is the Truth at work in my own existence. It is no abstract moral or philosophical proposition, but the disclosure of the vitality of God in this world. It is no self-induced, positive thought but involves risking death as the conclusive power in human experience and then and there being found by the grace of God in the midst of death. It may not be earned, nor sought; it is rather the drama of God proving Himself as God, showing Himself in the common affairs of men. It is no special possession or knowledge of my own, but it is the very event in which my own solidarity with every other man is constituted. It is that unequivocal assurance that I am loved by One who loves all others which enables me to love myself and frees me to love another, any other, every other.

Mind you, all this does not mean that the existence of crisis can be rationalized, or in any way minimized, or denied. Leave that to the sentimentalists and the stupid and the pietistic. Nor can crisis be easily simplified, as the mass evangelists of Protestantism suppose. Neither can crisis be ignored, nor regarded as an unfortunate embarrassment, as some ecclesiastical authorities vainly think. There is no place to hide from crisis — especially not in the Church of Christ; on the contrary, the making of a Christian anticipates the extreme and signal experience of crisis which is the exposure to death.

For what these anxieties which afflict and assail men in their ordinary lives foretell and even now represent is the concrete and profound reign of death in a man's own, immediate, actual life and circumstances and — at the same time and in the same event — the personal and decisive exposure to the presence of God which subdues death and ends death's reign once and for all.

In a sense, therefore, the existence of crisis in any man's
life conceals the mystery of Christ. Crisis — if we do not
hide from it or suppress it or flee it or become its victims —
is the visitation of death in our lives which holds the fact
that the life of God is stronger than death and embraces
human life and prevails over death in the specific history of a
man. Crisis — that is, the serious encounter of a man with
exactly that which now threatens his own life, with that which
represents, signifies and warns of his own death — is always
terrible, wonderful, eventually inescapable, saving and holy.

In other words, the most notorious, plain, and victorious
truth of God is that God participates in our history — even
yours and mine. Our history — all our anxieties — have become
the scene of His presence and the matter of His care. We
are safe. We are free. Wherever we turn we shall discover that God is already there. Therefore, wherever it be,
fear not, be thankful, rejoice, and boast of God.

The power to discern God's presence in common life is
imparted when one becomes a Christian, an event in which
the power of the Word of God in one's own personal history is manifest over and over against the power of death.
Then and thereafter the Christian lives in any and all events
in reliance upon the presence of the Word of God. Then
and thereafter the Christian lives to comfort other men,
whatever their afflictions, with the news of God's care for
the world. Then and thereafter the threat of his own eventual
historic death holds no fear for the Christian, for there is
nothing which he will on that day experience which he has
not already foretasted in the event of his becoming a Christian, in the event of his surrender to the power of death and
of his being saved from that power by the presence of
God. Then and thereafter he is free from the most elementary
and universal bondage of men: the struggle to maintain
and preserve, whatever the cost, his own existence against
that of all other men. Then and thereafter he is free to give
his present life away, since his life is secure in the life of God.

All this has been recited and observed in the Church in the
sacrament of Baptism, of course, since the earliest days of

Christian life. Yet it cannot be overlooked that Baptism is a much misunderstood and, ironically, since it is the most common experience of Christians, the most neglected of sacraments. It is regarded in a very perfunctory and cavalier fashion in many of the congregations of Protestantism. The obvious sign of that is the frequency with which it is placed in a context outside the corporate worship of a congregation and is thus degraded to a ritual of family life, involving only the immediate relatives and designated sponsors of a child. To find Baptism reduced to the mere observance of the natural birth of a child or to a ceremony for naming a child or to separate it from the center of the life of a congregation is especially anomalous in the instance of infant Baptism. For while, to put it succinctly, the responsible party to Baptism in the case of an adult convert to the Christian faith who is baptised is the convert now taking his place as a member of the Church; the responsible party in the case of the infant who is baptised but who is neither instructed in the Christian faith nor converted to the faith is the congregation. Not even the natural parents of the child have as much responsibility in this event as does the congregation and as do those designated as immediate representatives of the Church to the child, the godparents. In the case of the adult convert who is baptised, his Baptism is the public announcement to the world that he has been freed in his own life from the power of death by the grace of God for him and, therefore, joins the company of all baptised people, the Church, and covenants with his fellow members of the Church to serve the world by honoring God's presence in the world. But as for the infant who is baptised, his Baptism is the public proclamation to the world by the Church, and specifically of a congregation of the Church, of the faith of the Church, and concretely of the members of that congregation, in the power of God to raise the dead and of the care of God that this child, which at his birth death claimed, be saved from death. And this is proclaimed by the congregation in the Baptism of an infant out of the confidence in God's compassion for all men, a compassion to which the congregation is witness because of His concern for them. No more radical trust in God can be shown by a congregation of Christian people than when a child is baptised.

But how cheaply and frivolously it is observed in so many congregations! How absurd if the congregation is absent, as so often happens. How vulgar to tip a minister for presiding at a Baptism, as if this were not the very thing he is called and ordained to do. How ridiculous to hide this news from the public, when it is essentially news for the world. How fearful the churches are of the power and freedom of the Word of God in this world!

The Freedom of the Christian Life

The presence of God's Word in common life and the gift of discernment of that Word in the world mean a very radical freedom for Christians, and for the Church, in the world, and in the service of the world. There is no place in which that freedom may not be exercised, for there is no place in which the Word of God is absent. There is no time in which that freedom is restricted since the One the world awaits has already come.

The freedom of the Christian life and the service to the world accomplished when that freedom is exercised is not to be confused with conventional charity — with "doing good," with helping other people in the ordinary meaning of those words, with good works. In East Harlem, and elsewhere, I have seen a lot of conventional charity. East Harlem is virtually invested with social workers and voluntary and governmental agencies of all sorts, all heartily engaged in helping the people of the neighborhood with the rearing of children, the maintenance of marriages, the finding of jobs, the curbing of delinquency, the rehabilitation of addicts, the procurement of housing, the protection of tenants, and all the rest. Now I do not deprecate any of this, but it must be distinguished from the witness and service of Christians.

For one thing, the great peril in the notion that a man may intentionally do, and know that he is doing, good for

another man is that it preempts the office of God in judging
the actions and decisions of men. The man who claims for
his action toward another man that his action is good is in
the arrogant position of asserting that he knows already how
God will judge his act or decision.

Beyond that, however, is the further peril of tyrannizing the
one of whom it is said that he is being helped. The danger
is that in the reason for doing what is thought or said to
be good to another the one who has acted intends and feels
that he justifies himself. So the real issue, in such action, is
not the other's welfare, but your own; not his nurture, but
your justification. Notice, too, how often the standard of
help — rehabilitation, as it is usually called — is not just made
up of the common morality of middle class society, but
specifically in how far the client or patient or case imitates
and becomes like the case worker or probation person or
professional — that is, in how far the one who is being helped
becomes like the one who is helping him. This is a temptation present in any situation where some form of conventional charity is undertaken where there is a direct contact
between persons, as distinguished from conventional charity —
social work, counselling, medical care, and the like — organized on an impersonal and bureaucratic basis. And while
I am sympathetic with criticisms of the latter, for their de-
personalizing impact upon those who receive services, the
former instance may in fact involve a more terrible tyranny
of one person over another. I think a lot of people are
murdered in the name of the good which is done to them.

The Christian would, characteristically, be sensitive to these
temptations in conventional charity since he has no longer
any reason to be anxious about his own moral justification.
He knows that God judges as He will and that a man's
justification consists not in the good that he intends or does,
but in the mercy and grace of God. And the Christian is
concerned not so much with conventional charity, with
coping with human problems or social issues according to the
tradition of society, as with the representation in the life
of society, with all its human problems and social issues, of

the intercession of Christ for the whole of life and for every fragment of life.

One of the earliest clients that I had in East Harlem was a boy whom I will call Ramon. He came to me one night and said: "You're a lawyer — tell me what to do. The police are looking for me and I want to go into the Marines and I want to know what will happen if I do that or what will happen if I turn myself in to the police." He wanted to clear up the present chapter in his life before going on to a new life and wondered what he should do about the fact that the police wanted him for questioning. In investigating the matter, I discovered that the police were interested in questioning him about an incident that had taken place in the neighborhood some eighteen months prior to the time he came to me.

One night in the early summer, he and some of the other boys from his gang had been loitering on the street and a girl had come by whom some of the boys, although not my client, had taken up on the roof of a nearby tenement and there each of them committed what is legally called statutory rape, since the girl was legally not of the age of consent, but what is colloquially called in East Harlem a "line-up." Initially there were four boys involved. During the incident one of the boys came down and told Ramon that the girl wanted him to come to the roof, which he did, and he then also had intercourse with her. This was still, of course, statutory rape in Ramon's case, because of the girl's age, though she apparently had specifically consented to and, indeed, solicited him. Cases of this sort are not too frequently subject to police investigation or criminal prosecution unless some complaint is made or the matter somehow otherwise reaches the attention of the authorities. In this instance, the girl was hospitalized in the next few days, the hospital reported the matter, and so there was an investigation by the police. In due course the four boys involved in the original incident were picked up, but not Ramon. None of the boys arrested disclosed Ramon's name or whereabouts. Eventually the other boys were charged, tried, con-

victed, and imprisoned. Ramon knew that he was wanted
by the police and was shrewd enough to move from his
parent's tenement to a relative's home in an adjacent precinct.
And there he had remained ever since without being appre-
hended.

It seemed likely that Ramon could remain there indefinitely
without great jeopardy of being arrested, although there
would always be some risk of that. It also seemed clear that
if Ramon were picked up or if he surrendered to the police,
he would, like his friends, be tried and convicted and imprisoned.

While I was investigating the matter and wondering what
counsel to give to Ramon, I was visited by two people from
the neighborhood interested in Ramon and in this case. One
visitor was a seminarian who, as part of his field work assign-
ment, was working with the gang to which Ramon belonged,
coaching them in basketball. When the seminarian came to
me he said "I heard that Ramon has talked with you about
giving himself up to the police. That's the first time this
kid has shown any sense of responsibility about what happened with that girl or about much of anything else."
This, incidentally, was not the case, because within his
society, within his gang, Ramon had a very great sense of
responsibility, even though he may not have had much toward society outside his gang, toward society hostile to his
society. Anyway, the seminarian thought of Ramon as irresponsible and welcomed his consideration of surrendering
to the police as a sign of responsibility. But the seminarian
raised another consideration: he proposed that he and I, as
Christians, should so counsel with Ramon that there would be
precipitated, out of his anxiety about whether to give himself
up, a personal crisis, a repentance for what he had done, and,
hopefully, a traumatic conversion. Then, figured the seminarian, after Ramon becomes a Christian, after his conversion,
he will himself know what he should do about the police.

It all seemed very manipulative and a bit morbid, as I recall,
but the seminarian had, nevertheless, raised a serious issue,

that is, the primary concern for the evangelization of all men, including Ramon.

The second visitor was a minister from one of the neighborhood churches. He said that he had also heard of Ramon's visit to me and that I should know that "Ramon is a menace." The boy had gotten away with rape and, the minister alleged, though he had no legal proof, Ramon had also been involved in other "line-ups" from time to time that had never been investigated by the police, and had also been implicated in a robbery about which no police action had been taken. Ramon was increasingly lionized by his friends because of his skill or success in getting away with all this, according to the minister, and was therefore a bad influence on other boys. "For the good of society, for the good of the neighborhood," the minister proposed, "we should get him to turn himself in." And though, as a lawyer, I thought the minister less informed or concerned than he might have been, about the necessity to protect an accused person until his guilt is legally established, I acknowledge that he raised a significant issue, and one for which Christians have always had great concern, namely, the welfare and safety and order of society as a whole.

In spite of the issues raised by the seminarian and by the minister, I decided that my own advice to Ramon would be to join the Marines. Admittedly, there is perhaps not much choice between staying in East Harlem and risking arrest or some further trouble, or surrendering to the police and going to jail, or joining the Marines, but perhaps, if Ramon went into the military service he might learn something useful for later employment — a trade skill, or the improvement of his English, or the like — possibilities which were not in prospect either in remaining in East Harlem or in going to jail. Maybe there was a little better chance for his life if he took this course; both prison and East Harlem seemed to offer only more trouble for Ramon. And this was something he wanted himself to do, if he could.

Legally there was no impediment to his joining the Marines. He was wanted for questioning, but he had not been charged, indicted, convicted of any crime. Ramon was legally still innocent of any crime. When he joined the Marines he would have to sign a form under oath that he had not been indicted or convicted, and he could do this.

Ramon's self-interest seemed to be in entering the service.

The story of Ramon portrays something of the style of the Christian life and witness in the world. It points, for instance, to the fact that there is never an abstract, single "Christian answer" to an issue to which all Christians are bound to adhere or conform. On the contrary, the positions taken by the three Christians on the scene, implicated in one way or another in the actual case, the seminarian and the minister and myself, are all responsible Christian positions. Christians care that every man be evangelized, as the seminarian represented. Christians care for all of society, as the minister represented. Christians care for men in a radically individual sense and are free to advocate the cause of one, as in this case of Ramon, as over against everyone and everything else in the world.

The image of Christian action in the world is that of the people of God living in dispersion in the world and in any corner of the world, finding trustworthy God's promise that He cares for all men and for each man. Moreover, Christians are free in their dispersion to intercede for the cause of any man — even one who is said by others to be unworthy — and thereby to represent in the world the intercession of Christ for all men — even though none be worthy. The image of Christian witness in the world is that of a people who have so completely divested themselves of their own individual self-interest that they may intercede — stand in the place of, represent, advocate — the cause of another, any other at all. And then, now and again, the people return from their extraordinarily versatile involvement in the life of the world, to gather as the Church to represent, before God, the world out of which they have come, in all its concreteness and conflict and change, and to celebrate as the Church the presence of the Word of God as they have known it in the world.

The Church's Need of the World

If the life of the Church, either of the members dispersed in the world or of the gathered worshipping community, is to be an exercise of the power to discern the presence of the Word of God in common life and is to be a radically free and versatile involvement in the turmoil and travail of the world's everyday existence; if the life of the Church is to be intercessory; and if the Church is to be the servant of the world in the name and in the style of Christ, then Christians must live in the world — and not for their own sake, and not for the sake of the Church, much less for the sake of any of the churches, not even for God's sake, but for the sake of the world. That is to say, the Christian must live in this world, where Christ lives: he must live in this world *in* Christ.

Yet what Christians are faced with are churches, at least in Protestantism, which at every echelon of their existence — Sunday school, youth fellowships, vestries and sessions, agencies, councils, denominations, congregations and parishes, women's work, rummage sales, bingo games and coffee hours, sermons, seminaries, boy scouts, choirs and dial-a-prayers, bastard architecture, segregated premises, effete or effeminate images of Jesus, grossly inflated bureaucracies and all the rest — churches which are to a great extent separated from the world, afraid of the world, which feel unprepared, insecure, and inadequate for the mission of the Church in the world, and for whom the jargons of theological discussion or the examples of the clergy or the formalities of the practice of religion are no assurance or adequacy. These churches more and more retreat into themselves. They become so inverted, so caught up in internal maintenance and procedure, so entrapped in preserving and proliferating a cumbersome, costly, self-serving, officious, indulgent, soft ecclesiastical apparatus that it becomes easy to think that they don't have to care about the world any more since they are so much consumed in caring for themselves.

Nevertheless, it is when and where the churches are most estranged from and least involved in the common life of the world that the churches are the most worldly, and most resemble the worldly principalities and powers. The separation of the churches from the world, the superstition that the Word of God is or can be isolated from ordinary, everyday life, the preoccupations of the churches with conserving their own existence rather than serving the world — all these are the substance of estrangement from Christ. Where the churches do not care for the world, they do not really care for Christ.

I know a clergyman who was recently coerced into leaving his work in New York City because his ecclesiastical superiors informed him that his ministry was becoming "too specialized." He cared for the world and he spent his time in the world. The only time you could find him on the church premises was when he was presiding at worship. The rest of the time he could be found in the street, or in a home, or in a bar, or in the neighborhood political club, or at the precinct police station, or in a candy store, or in some other place where people are. But he was told that he spent too much time with people, especially with some who were junkies or prostitutes or colored or poor or otherwise "undesirable." What happened to him is a measure of how deeply estranged the churches are from the world — and from Christ. What happened to him is a sign of how embarrassing the Gospel has become to the churches.

Christians must enter the common life of the world fully and unequivocally in order to know the Word of God, in order to witness to the Word of God in the world, in order to worship God at all. The several churches, now becoming so audible about their concern for the reunion of the Church, must become and be deeply and passionately immersed in service to the world if the unity of the Body of Christ is to be recovered and restored. For the sake of Christian unity, the churches need the world because the Word of God is present in the world anyway and already. And Christians individually and the churches severally can be, should be, immersed in the world's life to the extremity of giving up their own present lives for the world's sake. For the "ecumenical movement" this is of enormous practical significance: in giving up their present lives for the world, Christians will learn of unity. They will discover how to give up their lives for each other and for a better life, for a new life, for a renewed life together.

The Fear of God

*Him we proclaim, warning every man and teaching every man
in all wisdom, that we may present every man mature in Christ.*

Colossians 1:28

THE MINISTRY OF THE CHURCH as the Body of Christ in the
world is the same as the ministry of Christ. The ministry
of Christ is the ministry of a servant in the world and for
the world — a servant of the world in the name of God.

Perhaps it is helpful to notice a few things about the
ministry of Christ. One is that the ministry of Christ is a
ministry of great extravagance — of a reckless, scandalous
expenditure of His life for the sake of the world's life. Christ
gives away His life. The world finds new life in His life and
in His gift of His life to the world. His is not a very prudential life, not a very conservative life, not a very cautious
life, not — by ordinary standards — a very successful life.

He shunned no one, not even adulterers, not even tax
collectors, not even neurotics and psychotics, not even those
tempted to suicide, not even alcoholics, not even poor people,
not even beggars, not even lepers, not even those who
ridiculed Him, not even those who betrayed Him, not even
His own enemies. He shunned no one.

The words that tell of the ministry of Christ are words of
sorrow, poverty, rejection, radical unpopularity. They are
words of agony.

It seems ridiculous to apply such words to the ministry of
churches nowadays. Yet where these words cannot be truth-
fully applied to the ministry of the churches today they must
then be spoken against the churches to show how far the
churches are from being the Body of Christ engaged in the
ministry of Christ in the world.

The Church exists as the company of participants in God's
witness to Himself in the world. The Church exists for the

sake of the world into which God enters and in which He acts and for which He expends His own life. One who is a participant in the Church, one who is incorporated into this Body, one who is baptised into this company has not only the personal freedom to expend his own life without guile or calculation or fear of death — or any more minor prudence — but also, characteristically, he is indifferent to whether or not the churches maintain an amiable reputation in society, or whether or not the churches have much wealth and a sound investment program, or whether or not the churches, or the ecclesiastical authorities, have much political influence. On the contrary, the Christian is suspicious of respectability and moderation and success and popularity. And this is so because the genius of the Christian life, both for a person and for the company of Christians, is the freedom constantly to be engaged in giving up its own life in order to give the world new life. All the questions of status and power and reputation, and all defensive, conservative and self-serving questions about preserving the institutional existence of the churches are matters of some indifference except insofar as they impede the ministry of the Body of Christ, entice men into false religion and a wrong understanding of what the Christian society is, and lure them into misleading notions of what the Christian life is all about.

How much or how often the churches are engaged in serving themselves instead of the world, that is, how far they have withdrawn from the ministry of the Body of Christ, are matters of practical consequence. For example, I had one day to fly to Boston to visit the Harvard Business School to give a lecture. I was late (some friends would say, as usual) in leaving my apartment to get out to the airport. Just as I was about to go, the telephone rang. I had not the will power not to answer it, in spite of my rush. It was a clergyman who was calling. "I have a woman in my office," he told me, "who is going to be evicted in the morning. Tell me what to do for her." I asked him a few questions and, as it turned out, the grounds for the eviction were the non-payment of the rent. The woman apparently had no money to pay her rent. She had, or asserted that she had, certain complaints against the landlord, but the complaints that she had were not sufficient, assuming that they could be legally established, to justify non-payment of the rent. They were no defense to the eviction, and if she wished to pursue them it would have to be done in a separate action against the landlord, apart from the eviction proceeding. By this time I was even more anxious about catching the airplane and said to the minister, "Well, sell one of your tapestries and pay the rent," and hung up and caught the plane. On the plane I thought the telephone conversation over and thought that perhaps I had been rude and too abrupt in answering the minister that way and I considered calling him back after landing to apologize. But by the time the plane landed at Logan Airport I had rejected that idea. My answer had not been rude or irresponsible. On the contrary, exactly what he and the people of his congregation, which does have several beautiful and valuable tapestries, must be free to do is to sell their tapestries to pay the rent — to pay somebody else's rent — to pay anybody's rent who can't pay their own rent. If they have *that* freedom, then, but only then, does the tapestry have religious significance; only then does the tapestry enrich and contribute to and express and represent the concern and care which Christians have in the name of God for the ordinary life of the world. The tapestry hanging in a church becomes and is a wholesome and holy thing, an appropriate and decent part of the scene of worship, only if the congregation which has the tapestry is free to take it down and sell it in order to feed the hungry or care for the sick or pay the rent or in any other way serve the world. The tapestry is an authentically Christian symbol only when it represents the freedom in Christ to give up any aspect of the inherited and present life of the institutional church, including, but not limited to, possessions, for the sake of the world.

The churches in America have many possessions, tapestries and otherwise, which they can have and hold with integrity in any Christian sense only insofar as they are free to give them up for the world as a witness to the ministry of Christ, as a sign of dying in Christ, as an honoring of the Word of God.

Ironically, this sort of freedom from possessions and property, but just as much, also, from considerations of reputation and status and political power and the like, is by no means an issue just for the churches in the affluent sectors of American society. It is a very serious issue as well for churches in the slums, in the inner city. There the churches, for the most part, have supposed that the inner city must become much more like the outer city before the Gospel can be heard. They have thought that mission follows charity. They have favored social reform and causes and crusades and postponed mission. I am all for changing the face of East Harlem and similar neighborhoods, but the mission of the Church depends not upon social reformation in these neighborhoods, as desperately as that is needed, but upon the presence of the Word of God in the society of the poor as it is right now. If the mere Gospel is not a whole salvation for the most afflicted man, it is no comfort to other men in less affliction. Mission does *not* follow charity. Faith does not follow works either for donor or recipient; on the contrary, mission is itself the only charity which Christians have to offer the poor, the only work which Christian have to do.

The premise of most urban church work, it seems, is that in order for the Church to minister among the poor, the Church has to be rich, that is, to have specially trained personnel, huge budgets, many facilities, rummage to distribute, and a whole battery of social services. Rather, the opposite is the case. The Church must be free to be poor in order to minister among the poor. The Church must trust the Gospel enough to come among the poor with nothing to offer the poor except the Gospel, except the power to discern and the courage to expose the Gospel as it is already mediated in the life of the poor.

When the Church has the freedom itself to be poor among the poor, it will know how to use what riches it has. When the Church has that freedom, it will know also how to minister among the rich and powerful. When the Church has that freedom, it will be a missionary people again in all the world. When the Church has the freedom to go out into the world with merely the Gospel to offer the world, then it will know how to use whatever else it has — money and talent and buildings and tapestries and power in politics — as sacraments of its gift of its own life to the world, as tokens of the ministry of Christ.

The Prudence of the Churches

Nowadays it is not this sort of freedom which marks the churches, but the prudence of putting, as the first consideration in any event, the institutional preservation of the churches, the consolidation of their present situation. It does not happen very often within the American churches that a tapestry has to be sold to pay somebody's rent, but the churches here are of no mind even to contemplate such an action. This appears to be the case at places in the life of the churches even where one might expect or hope for a modest radicality and a less entrenched vested interest in maintaining everything the way it is and has been.

The student movement, for instance, in the churches of Protestantism, which once had very great freedom in discussion and at least a flair, if not any more than that, for action, seems more and more, in my observation of it and contact with it, on dead center — immobilized, as it has been, in its preoccupation with internal organizational and institutional issues. The turning point, in my view, for the student movement, the place at which it turned from a lively and venturesome enterprise and into another fragment of the ecclesiastical bureaucracy came when the National Student Christian Federation became a part of the National Council of Churches.[1] Now, the National Council is criticized fre-

1. The National Student Christian Federation embraces the major denominational student movements in this country, along with the Interseminary Movement and the Student Volunteer Movement for Christian Missions. It became affiliated with the National Council of Churches in 1960.

quently, but for the wrong reasons. The charges about it being radical politically remain unsubstantiated for the simple reason that they cannot be substantiated. The criticism that can be substantiated about the National Council and the reason that has substance for concern is that it represents the most unstable ecclesiastical bureaucracy in existence. That is to say, the National Council, having no real constituency, being a mere assembly of representatives of divided and independent denominations, is bound to be concerned, as the first and if necessary the only order of business, with how to keep itself going. And pretty soon its reason for existence becomes — not service to the world, not ecumenical studies and relationships, not witness within the public life of American society, not the reunion of the Church — but its existence. And, I fear, though in this I would gladly be proved wrong, that now the student movement becomes chained to this same debilitating and decadent process at work in American Protestantism.

The chief evidence of health in the student movement within the past few years has been its participation in and identification with the civil rights struggle, specifically with the "sit-in movement." Though very many students were involved in them, and though many of those so involved are Christian students, the sit-in demonstrations were not originated in the student Christian movement. But the student Christian movement participated in the sit-ins, conferred and collaborated with other student organizations implicated in them, raised some funds for defense of students arrested, and altogether took a significant and useful and honorable and active part in the sit-ins. (In the irony of God it may be that the sit-ins — a work and witness in the world — saved the vitality of the student Christian movement in this country from the threat that it would just be defeated, wither and expire in the wilderness of the ecclesiastical bureaucracy to which it has attached itself.)

But the participation of the student Christian movement in the sit-ins was cautious and prudential enough, all the same. There was a meeting, at the time the sit-in demonstrations were beginning to gain momentum, of a number of students and leaders from the student Christian movement to consider the role of Christian students in the sit-ins and to discuss whether Christian students had any particular responsibilities in the crisis over segregation in this country. It occurred to someone planning the meeting that the sit-ins involved issues of law and theology as well as political tactics, and I was invited to attend the meeting to make some comments about civil disobedience in the light of both American law and of the Christian faith. I listened to their discussions about the sit-ins that had taken place in lunch counters, and about the prospects for similar demonstrations in libraries and public beaches and other facilities.

Then a few people in the meeting raised the issue of the integration of local congregations. It was pointed out that this was an issue common in the North as well as the South, since most congregations in both regions remain segregated. And some thought that Christian students ought particularly to be concerned with this, and that, indeed, even if the public policy of the land did not happen to favor integration, Christians would still, because of the new relationships and the new community into which men enter in Baptism, characteristically belong to integrated congregations.

After a long discussion about why Christian students specifically had a responsibility in respect to integrating congregations, the talk turned to specific situations in certain cities in the North and in the South where it was known there are segregated congregations but where there also are, in nearby colleges, integrated campus Christian groups. It was proposed that in places where these facts pertained the members of the integrated campus Christian groups should present themselves to the local segregated congregations, hoping through discussion or negotiation with the local church people, and through demonstrations — kneel-ins, perhaps — if necessary, to bring about the integration of these congregations.

But then it dawned on somebody what would happen if this course of action were undertaken. If these students from

integrated campus Christian groups presented themselves
to local congregations and asked for membership and were
accepted and thereby integration began in these congregations,
why then these students would have really to become and be
responsible members of the congregations, at least as long
as they lived in that community. It would not be like sitting-
in at a lunch counter, where you might go and demonstrate
and win the right for anybody to buy a cup of coffee there,
but where you would never necessarily have to return your-
self to patronize the place after the right was secured. Not
so in integrating congregations. There you would have to
come, and demonstrate, and *stay* and enter fully into the
common life of the congregation. And this would mean that
since the students would become integrated, not only racially,
but as students, into the local congregation, there would
not be much reason any more for the campus Christian groups
from which the students had come. This course of action
aimed at integrating congregations might well mean that the
campus groups would have to give up their own existence
for the sake of the broader unity of the Church in that
place. And then awful things would follow. Some chaplains
or campus Christian workers would no longer have jobs, and
the leaders of the student Christian movement might have no
movement to lead. The threat was that these Christian students would have to give up their present mode of life and
present institutional form for the sake of a new life.

The discussion stopped right there. The consideration of
committing the student Christian movement in a deliberate
and serious way to the integration of local congregations
ended as soon as a glimpse was caught of what it might cost,
as soon as it appeared that it might mean losing life in the
hope of finding life, and in the hope of giving life to others.
And so, unto this day, there are many integrated campus
Christian groups in colleges around the country in both the
North and the South, and, if you look near by, you will commonly find segregated congregations.

Prudence, the anxiety to conserve and preserve their own
lives, rather than the freedom to expend their lives in the

manner of the ministry of Christ, is the temper that prevails in the churches of Protestantism.

The Recognition of Christ's Ministry in the World

The caution of the churches toward practicing the ministry of Christ in the world, the fear of the churches of losing their present lives, the preoccupations of the churches with status, security, and success — all of that does not keep the world from understanding and recognizing what the ministry of Christ in the world truly is and, therefore, from knowing what the ministry of the Church should characteristically be. Where the Christians are untrue or confused in their calling and witness, the world is not thereby prevented from comprehending the service owed to the world by the Church. The world may not be fond of the Gospel, the world may reject Christ, but the very presence of the Word of God in the world, the very witness of God to Himself in the common life of the world, informs the world of that which the world rejects, of that which the world hates. That is why, incidentally, the accommodations of the churches to the world, the appeasement and compromises by which the churches equivocate in their witness and mission in the world are vain. Perhaps the Gospel does not please the world, but the world has insight into that in the Gospel which is unpleasing to the world, and that means that the Gospel only incurs a further displeasure and derision of the world when the churches expose their own discomfort with and distrust of the Gospel.

There is, among my friends and clients, for instance, a boy who is a narcotics addict. He is now in prison for the sixth time for an offense related to his addiction. His conviction this time involved a theft from a church, a place which is, in my observation as a lawyer, the very last place one should steal from, not because of its being a church, but because there will be little chance of leniency in such a case, since the police and the courts have a rather protective attitude toward the churches, and since it seems to be difficult for a church to forgive an offense against its property. Anyway, my friend is in prison again, this time with a very stiff sentence. I have defended him in some of his difficulties with the law. He often visits me when he is free, and we have talked a lot together. I am not aware that I have ever told him that he has a bad and costly and very debilitating habit. He knows that better than I do. And while he and I have talked about how his habit might be controlled or even cured, our relationship is not contingent upon his breaking his addiction. Acceptance of another person is acceptance of the other as he is, without entailing any demands that he change in any empirical way. This boy is an addict, and while I would rejoice if he were freed from this affliction, that would not change or increase my acceptance of him as a person. And though I am not an addict, that makes me no better nor any worse than he. I am not his judge. I am just his friend.

On the last occasion when he was released from prison, he returned, at the behest of his father, who loves him, though he is prodigal, to Puerto Rico. His father had in mind that perhaps if his son got out of East Harlem for awhile, got away from the place and environment within which he had first become addicted and where many of his companions are addicts and where drugs are so readily available, he would be able to be cured.

Now this boy, who is one of the heaviest addicts that I have known, has had as much attention to his addiction problem as is imaginable or available. Social workers have counselled him, psychiatrists, and clergy, and vocational guidance people, and lawyers, and medical doctors all have been involved in his case. He has twice been in the Federal narcotics hospital, and once in a local narcotics hospital facility. Everything that is known that can be done for an addict has been done for him. He is still an addict, and his addiction deepens terribly as time goes on.

But his father has not renounced him or given up hope. He

arranged for him to go to Puerto Rico, found a job for him
there, and a place for him to live.

Now, just before the boy was to leave to go to Puerto
Rico, a clergyman, one who had spent an enormous amount
of time working with and trying to help this boy over the
years, wrote a letter to a fellow minister in Puerto Rico, a
minister whom he had reason to believe the boy would turn
to if he needed assistance while in the island. The letter
reported that the boy was on his way there and also that
the New York minister and some of his colleagues had worked
with the boy for many years and had finally come to the
conclusion that the boy is a hopeless case and cannot be
rehabilitated. Probably, by the way, the minister is correct
in this conclusion; clinically speaking, the boy is most likely
going to die an addict. Since the boy is a hopeless case, the
letter continued, the minister had decided, for the sake of the
work with other addicts for whom there was still some hope
of rehabilitation, to extend no further assistance to this
boy, and he advised his correspondent, the clergyman in
Puerto Rico, not to help the boy, and especially not to give
him any money, should the boy ask for assistance while in
Puerto Rico.

Sometimes clergymen are not too practical and overlook
obviously important facts. In this instance the minister writ-
ing this letter overlooked the fact, or perhaps he did not know
the fact, that the girl in his office who typed the letter is
sometimes the lover of the boy in question. So, of course,
she told the boy about the letter, and the boy knew he had
been designated a hopeless case.

After awhile, the boy returned to New York City. He
came one Sunday afternoon to visit me and told me about
the letter and talked for fully three hours about this incident
and about what it meant to him. And the burden of what
he said was this: if somebody goes, in a neighborhood like
East Harlem, to a welfare agency, or to a hospital, or to a
settlement house, or the like, he knows in advance what

services will be extended by the agency. They state what services are available and the terms under which they are available. If you qualify, if you fit into the categories established to qualify for the service, then you wait your turn and receive the service. It is all fair and square. You know where you stand. But, he said, it is different with the Church. It is different if some come to such a neighborhood and declare that they are Christians. If they say that, if they represent that they are Christians, then that means, my friend said, that "they are at my disposal." He understood that even if it is clinically true that he is a hopeless addict, this does not terminate his access to the Church nor the expendability of the life of the Church for him and for his life.

Now I do not relate this episode in order to denounce the minister involved, and I repeat that I concur, from my own observation, in the conclusion that the boy is probably hopelessly addicted. But the boy has better theological insight in this case than the clergyman. I seem, indeed, to recollect a word in the New Testament about hopeless cases, about leaving the many to find the one who is lost. The doctrine of ministry represented by the minister's letter seems, on the contrary, to be abandonment of the lost to stay with the many.[2]

The boy here knows this, knows something about what the ministry of Christ in the world is like, knows something, too, about how it differs from the conventional charities of secular agencies and institutions, knows that the representation by a church or individual of being Christian means the radical expendability of Christians within and on behalf of the world. And the boy knows this even where some lesser, some more restrained, some equivocal representation has been made by Christians to him about their expendability for him and for the life of the world.

The world recognizes the ministry of Christ even though and even where and when it is not the ministry practiced by Christians or by the churches.

2. Cf. Matthew 18:12-14.

The Ministry of Christ and the Fear of God

Now and then, however, the freedom which Christians are given as ministers of Christ, even to the extremity of giving up their present life, and in that event finding life and offering new life to the world, is known and exercised. Now and then, thereby, the world is reassured that what it looks for and recognizes as the integrity and style of that ministry is that which it can indeed expect and look forward to from Christians.

Now and then some Christian risks his life upon the Gospel, and in such events it becomes known in the world that the ministry of Christ lives. At such times the churches are recalled to that ministry.

A friend of mine is such a Christian. He had had some kind of depressing, conventional, un-Christian Sunday School background, but when he became a man and went to the university and entered upon his life's work, he left these things behind. He had become a graduate student, working for a Ph.D. in English literature. (Often one has to do apparently ridiculous things to get a Ph.D. My friend was engaged, for example, in preparing a thesis on the meaning of laughter in sixteenth-century English literature.) After a time, he began to grow restless and a bit hostile toward this work, and toward what he regarded as the excessive pedantry and apparent irrelevance of his studies. While he was laboring away at this exercise, becoming all the time more and more skeptical about it, he happened to go one night to the play "J.B." In it reference is made somewhere to the laughter of God. After he saw this play he began looking through the Bible to find instances where God laughs or where reference is made to His laughter. I suppose this was a way to ridicule his Ph.D. work, or anyway to keep it in perspective. He used to call me from time to time to tell me about some instance of God's laughter that he had uncovered in the Bible. Sometimes he would speculate, too, on the sort of things which provoke God's laughter, or the sound of God's laughter, or, more broadly, he would discuss God's sense of humor.

But what began as, I suppose, a facetious exercise, did not very long remain one, for God really *does* have a sense of humor. You see, there are not very many instances of God's laughter, or related allusions, in the Bible, and consequently, in his diligent, if somewhat whimsical search, my friend read a great deal of the Bible and, gradually, the Bible came alive to him. The cause of my friend changed. He was no longer so much exploring the mystery of God's laughter as listening to and hearing the Word of God in the Bible. His telephone calls, and conversations, changed. He would call and say, "You ought to look at this," and cite a passage, and then report what he had heard it say, not what he thought of it particularly, but just what was being uttered, what was being said, what he heard. He would just call to report the news which he had heard. He would never bother with the usual telephone talk — inquiring about my health, or commenting on the events of the day, or what not. He would just report the news, and then hang up.

He learned the most essential thing about the relationship between a reader and the Bible. He had learned to listen to the Bible; he had discovered that to hear the Word of God in the Bible a man must be ready to listen — to give himself to the Bible, asking only the question *What is being said?* There are other uses of the Bible, and I am not denouncing them. There is a place for treating the Bible as literature, there is a place and responsibility for Biblical criticism, there is a sense in which the Bible is history, and it is of some importance and help to know as much as can be known about the historical context in which a book or letter of the Bible was written, and who the writer was, and so on. And there are other more personal questions that may be asked of the Bible, or of a particular portion or passage of the Bible — such as whether the Word uttered and now heard in the Bible is confirmed in one's own experience, or in the contemporary life of the world. No one going to the Bible needs to leave, or should leave, any of his own experience or faculties behind. Let him, on the contrary, go to the

Bible with all that he has in his own knowledge and intelligence and feeling and common sense. But, before all of that, before any of that can be useful and honest and edifying, a man must first give himself to *merely* listening to the Bible, to only the questions, *What is being said? What is the Word?* There can be no response, nor rejection, nor dialogue with the Bible unless and until a man has heard the Bible. And this is what my friend had found. He had listened to the Bible. He had heard the Word of God in the Bible.

I know of no Christian who has not had the same sort of experience; indeed, a man is constituted in his freedom as a Christian in the event of his hearing the Word of God in the Bible and in the company of the Church and, as well, in the common life of the world.

My friend's life began to change as he matured in the freedom of the Christian life, as he became more and more immersed in the Word of God. He knew that his freedom meant that he was able to do any work in the world and that it could be a witness. He did not have to be a Ph.D. And in his freedom, he renounced his Ph.D. program. He had been studying under a fellowship — from a foundation, by the way, that boasts of its religious interest and emphasis — and he told the foundation that he was giving up his fellowship. The foundation wrote back a long letter which, in substance, said "You must be sick, and we hope you will get well, and if you get well quickly enough you can have the fellowship back." He looked for a job, and the job that he found was that of an orderly in a hospital, on the night shift, where his work was emptying bed pans, wrapping up dead bodies, and doing all the other things which orderlies have to do.

You never met a more emancipated man. He had come to know his freedom in Christ and had learned how to practice his freedom in Christ in the world.

And after quite awhile he came to understand that his freedom meant that he could indeed do anything, engage in any work, go anywhere, in the confidence and enjoyment of the presence of God in the world, as a member of the ministry of Christ in the world, including returning to the very place and work which he had given up. He could go back and finish his Ph.D. and even accept the fellowship, because he knew now that the integrity and efficacy of his own life and of his service in the world in the name of Christ is not dependent upon a particular place or work. He could return to his former work because now it had no longer any power to tyrannize his life. He was free, no longer in bondage to it. He had, in listening to the Word of God in the Bible, learned about losing his life and in that way finding his life. And the new life which he has found is a life which is at the disposal of the world.

In the end, what distinguishes the Christian faith from mere religion, what sets apart the practice of the Christian life from religiosity in any of its forms, what distinguishes the self-serving prudence of many of the churches of Protestantism from the freedom of participation in the ministry of Christ in the world, is the fear of God.

The fear of God in the Christian faith is the unanimous and elementary knowledge of the Church that *God is God.* The fear of God is grounded in the spontaneous response of a man to the active presence of the Word of God in the common life of the world, including the life of an ordinary man. The fear of God means the insight given to men into that which distinguishes God as, at once, wholly other than man and the world — free from humanity and the world, and yet, in His freedom as God, wholly intimate with men and this world — volunteering His love for the world, entering and acting in this history, giving His life to the world.

The fear of God, thus, is the initiation of worship. For the fear of God confesses the integrity and freedom of God and negates all substitutes for God, be they ideologies, or superstitions, or religious institutions, or nations, or the ordinary lusts of men. The fear of God confesses the freedom of God, and that is the beginning of freedom for men. That is the beginning of the ethics of redemption in which men are emancipated from the struggle to justify themselves. Now the dread of death is dissipated, since God, and not death, reigns. And now, at last, men are free to be men.

ACKNOWLEDGEMENTS

In one form or another, some material published here first appeared in The Christian Century, The Witness *and* The Episcopalian, *or was introduced in addresses at the University of Rochester, Amherst College, Duke University, and The North American Ecumenical Youth Assembly.*

WILLIAM STRINGFELLOW is a lawyer and an Episcopal layman, who is a frequent contributor to both legal and theological journals. After his graduation from the Harvard Law School, he practiced some years in the East Harlem neighborhood in New York City. He has been a visiting lecturer at several law schools and was one of six "young American theologians" to participate in a public dialogue with Karl Barth during Barth's visit to the United States.